M000248882

CONTENTS

INTRODUCTION

Frying is a common cooking method; it is quick easy, and tasty. Many restaurants and fast food chains use deep-frying as an economical and quick way to prepare foods. Honestly, everybody likes the taste of popular deep-fried foods such as fish sticks, French fries, chicken nuggets, doughnuts, and so on. Mmm, that is oh so delicious! Fatty foods taste so good! Unfortunately, deep-fried food is not good for your health. Deep fried foods tend to be high in calories and trans- fats, which can have negative effects on your weight and overall health.

However, you don't have to sacrifice flavor when trying to eat healthier and shed a few pounds. You should find another solution. An Air Fryer is a unique kitchen device designed to fry food in a healthy way. The Air Fryer cooks food with super-heated air that is circulated by high-powered fans, delivering that crispy, golden-brown exterior and a moist and tender interior. In other words, hot air is a new oil!

Let's say you want to prepare fish and chips. Instead of soaking your favorite food in a quart of hot cooking oil (which was probably GMO refined and old) in your regular pan, you can cook it with a tablespoon or two of healthy olive oil, and get a crispy, delicious food. Best of all – fried food does not taste like the fat. The Air Fryer cuts calories, not flavor! It makes cooking at home easy, quick, and most importantly – healthy!

Things to Know Before you Buy an Air Fryer

An Air Fryer is a kitchen appliance that utilizes super-heated air to cook food in a special chamber using the convection mechanism. Technically speaking, a mechanical fan blows heat around the space so the hot air circulates around your food at high speed, cooking evenly from all sides, producing crispy browning results. This is called the Maillard effect. According to Wikipedia "The Maillard reaction (/maɪˈjɑːr/ my-YAR; French: [majaʁ]) is a chemical reaction between amino acids and reducing sugars that gives browned food its distinctive flavor. Seared steaks, pan-fried dumplings, cookies and other kinds of biscuits, bread, toasted marshmallows, and many other foods undergo this reaction. It is named after French chemist Louis-Camille Maillard, who first described it in 1912 while attempting to reproduce biological protein synthesis."

This simple but intelligent machine radiates heat from heating elements and uses rapid air technology to fry roast, and bake your food with less oil. The Air Fryer can also warm your food. You don't have slave over a hot stove since the Air Fryer features an automatic temperature control. Thanks to its convection settings, it produces crispier and more flavorful food than conventional cooking methods.

If you are thinking of cutting down on fat consumption, here is a great solution. Studies have shown that air fried veggies contain up to 80% less fat in comparison to veggies that are deep fried. Just to give you an idea of the calorie content – deep-fried onion rings contain about 411 Calories vs air fried that contain about 176 Calories. Deep-fried Chicken Nuggets = 305 calories vs air fried = 180 Calories.

In order to understand how to use an Air Fryer, it would be good to find out more about the anatomy of this magical device. As we said before, there is the inside i.e. electric-coil heating elements. A specially designed fan distributes the hot air evenly throughout the cooking basket. Then, the Air Fryer has a removable cooking basket with a mesh bottom that is coated with a non-stick material. It is placed in a frying basket drawer, cooking your food in the sealed environment. When it comes to the features of an Air Fryer, it has a Control Dials – Temperature Control Dial and 60 Minute Countdown Timer Dial. You can use the preset time and temperature, or increase and decrease the cooking time and temperature to suit your recipe. Timer and buzzer are amazing features since you do not have to worry about overcooking or undercooking your food.

Air Fryers come with accessories, such as baking dishes, pans, trays, grill pans, skewer racks, and so forth; it will vary from model to model. However, make sure to use pans and racks that are designed to fit into the Air Fryer.

10 Air Fryer Tips You Should Know

Although an Air Fryer is easy to use, please follow these tips for getting the most out of your new, fancy device. Once you get into it, crispy and delicious foods are just minutes away!

How to keep the rendered fat drippings from burning? Simply pour a little water into the bottom of the air fryer drawer. In this way, the fat drippings can't reach smoking temperatures.

If you miss the traditional fried food, try melting butter and sprinkling in your favorite herbs and spices to shake things up. Then, you can whip up a healthy avocado mayo and a few drizzles of hot sauce for a custom dip. You can use a tablespoon or two of extra-virgin olive oil and add whatever aromatics you like (garlic, herbs, chili, etc.); the result is veggies with a crisp texture and fewer calories. Win-win!

As for cooking times, always test your food for doneness before removing it from the cooking chamber, even if you are an experienced cook. As for meats and poultry, use a meat thermometer to ensure that meat is cooked thoroughly. As its name implies, our Air Fryer Cooking Guide is intended as a guide only. The quantity and quality of food, as well as its thickness or density, may affect actual cooking time. It is recommended to cook food in smaller batches for the best results. Remove the frying basket drawer halfway through the cooking time to check your food. Most foods need to be shaken or turned over several times during the cooking time.

How to achieve that delicious, crispy surface? Pat your food dry before adding spices and oil. A tablespoon or two of oil should be brushed onto foods; experts recommend using oil sprays or misters with your favorite oil (olive, vegetable, or coconut oil). Avoid aerosol spray cans because they have harsh agents that can damage the coating on Air Fryer baskets.

Although most foods need some oil to help them crisp, there are certain foods that naturally have some fat such as fatty cuts of meat; therefore, you do not have to add extra fat to these foods, but anyway, do not forget to grease the cooking basket.

Allow your food to rest for 5 to 10 seconds before removing them from the cooking basket unless the recipe indicates otherwise.

Most of Air Fryer's manufactures specify that the unit should be preheated. However, it is not necessary every time. Simply set your Air Fryer to the desired temperature and wait for 3 to 5 minutes before putting your food into the cooking basket.

If you want to shake or add ingredients during the cooking cycle, simply remove the cooking basket; the machine will automatically shut down. Place the cooking basket back into the Air Fryer drawer and the cooking cycle will automatically resume.

Use your Air Fryer to reheat leftovers by setting the temperature to 300 degrees F for up to 10 minutes.

For crunchy, bright cruciferous vegetables, you can place them in boiling water for 3 to 5 minutes before adding them to the Air Fryer basket. Lightly toss your veggies with olive oil or an herbed vinaigrette and place in the preheated Air Fryer basket. Always remember not to over-fill the cooking basket. It is also important to keep air-fried veggies warm until ready to serve.

As for French fries, baking this favorite food is much healthier cooking method than deep-frying. Here's the secret to perfect fries. Cut your potatoes into 1/4-inch lengthwise pieces; make sure that the pieces are of uniform size; now, soak them in cold water for 30 minutes (45 minutes for sweet potato fries). You can add the vinegar to the water as well. Your fries will turn out slightly crispier and vinegar can improve their flavor too. When ready to eat, drain and pat them dry with a kitchen towel. Choose oil with a high smoke point such as olive oil, canola oil or clarified duck fat; when you're making sweet potato fries, coconut oil is an excellent choice because it will give a unique flavor to your favorite fries. Try not to crowd the fries in the Air Fryer basket. Afterwards, place them on a cooling rack set over a baking sheet – it is a little trick to keep your fries crispy until ready to serve. Salt your fries while they are still hot. Needless to say, use the best ingredients you can find.

7 Mistakes to Avoid with Your Air Fryer

Here are seven common mistakes people make when using Air Fryers – and how to avoid them.

You don't read instructions before beginning. When using an electrical appliance, basic manufacturer's instructions should always be followed; this is extremely important for safety reasons. That way, you'll avoid common mistakes.

You tend to overcrowd basket. We have said it before, and we'll say it again: If you tend to overcrowd the cooking basket, you're not allowing the Air Fryer to do its job properly. Crispy and slightly browned veggies are much more appealing and tasty than ones that are mushy and pale because of overcrowding. Therefore, for better results, give your food some breathing room in the cooking basket. Work in a few batches, and if you're in a hurry, cook smaller pieces of food. Larger Air Fryers can make the cooking process a little easier; keep that in mind if you are considering buying a new kitchen appliance. Anyway, never fill the Air Fryer basket more than 80% capacity.

You cook too small and lightweight items. As we said before, an Air Fryer has a powerful fan on top of the unit. It is not suitable for foods such as egg roll wrappers and lightweight freeze-dried foods, so be careful.

Your foods turn out dry and tasteless. Foods can dry out quickly on high temperatures; they can also come out stuck together. If your veggies turn out limp and mushy, this is a timing issue. Therefore, you should modify the temperature and time for certain food. If you are not sure, simply go 30 degrees F below and cut the time by 20 to 30 percent. Then, check your food and increase the cooking time if necessary.

You do not want to invest in some accessories. Accessories such as baking pans and oven-safe dishes have to be able to fit inside the cooking basket. Another important rule – they shouldn't come into contact with the heating element.

You're using wet coatings. Do not worry, wet battered foods such as tempura can be adapted to the Air Fryer. Coat your food generously with a crisp coating like breadcrumbs, crushed crackers, crushed tortilla chips, or pork rinds. Try to apply a classic three-step breading procedure (flour, eggs, and breadcrumbs) to reduce splattering.

You are afraid of mistakes. Mistakes are natural; they are also a big part of how we learn. Give yourself enough time to learn and enjoy a new cooking method. Remember, there is a time to plant and a time to harvest. Recipes can't be rushed if you want a delicious, perfectly cooked food.

Converting Traditional Recipes to the Air Fryer

Any ingredient that can be cooked in a microwave, conventional, convection, or toaster oven can be cooked in the Air Fryer. Simply put, air frying is just like baked and fried food in one. However, everything has its pros and cons so one of biggest disadvantages of Air Fryers is that they are smaller than standard ovens. Your favorite dinner, such as roasted meat with potatoes usually take 1 hour in the standard oven; it will take only 40 minutes in the Air Fryer. Add to this that instead of having to submerge ingredients in a lot of oil to make them flavorful and crispy, you will need a tablespoon or two of healthy vegetable oil.

Keep in mind that the heat in the Air Fryer is more intense than a conventional oven, so reduce the temperature by 25 to 50 degrees F. Slightly adjust the time by cooking your food for 20 to 30 percent less time. If you are not sure, simply start with less time and gradually adjust. Some authors recommend starting by cutting the time in half since the Air Fryer is much smaller than a conventional oven, so the heat is delivered inside the cooking basket more efficiently. What does it look like in practice?

If your recipe calls for roasting in the oven at 400 degrees F for 40 minutes, instead you should cook your food in the Air Fryer at 370 degrees F for about 30 minutes. Try using the cooking charts below to help determine the right cooking time for certain foods. Our chart features favorite Air Fryer foods, so that if you do not feel like reading recipes, then you can quickly check this list. Typically, most foods will cook at 360 to 380 degrees F; if you want ingredients more crispy, then cook them at 400 degrees F; if you want to slow cook your food, simply use lower temperatures. You can also try an online Air Fryer Calculator, which will easily convert oven guideline cooking temperatures and times to Air Fryer cooking times and temperatures. You can also find plenty of information about the Air Fryer frozen food times and temperatures. It includes favorite items like frozen chicken wings, shrimp, fries, mozzarella sticks, corn dog, fish sticks, hash browns, burritos, chicken tenders, pastries, tater tots, and so on.

Remember to check your foods for doneness. As with all cooking methods, it makes sense to open the lid and check the foods as they cook. Just remember to turn your food over halfway through the cooking time. As for small items like fries, you should test them every 5 to 10 minutes during cooking time. The same rule applies to packaged foods. And last but not least, it is incredibly important to choose the right size of the Air Fryer (the cooking baskets measure from 2 to 5.8 quarts). As you can see, using the Air Fryer isn't rocket science.

The Benefits of Using an Air Fryer

Health. Is the air frying a healthy cooking method? Deep fried foods absorb fat, which significantly increases their calorie content. Furthermore, these foods are typically coated in breadcrumbs, flour, or eggs prior to frying. For instance, a medium-sized baked potato (approximately 100 grams) contains about 93 calories, 0 grams of fat and 0 milligrams of cholesterol. On the other hand, 100 grams of French fries contain 319 calories and 17 grams of fat; they also contain high amounts of trans-fats and sodium (approximately 234 milligrams).

In fact, you should not be afraid of fat, you should avoid a harmful fat in a deep fryer oil that contains free radicals. Vegetable oils to avoid include soybean oil, corn oil, cottonseed oil, sunflower oil, peanut oil, and rice bran oil. Oils with health benefits include olive oil, coconut oil, grapeseed oil, flaxseed oil, avocado oil, walnut oil, and sesame oil. Butter, tallow, and lard are excellent for frying because they have a high smoke point. Unfortunately, healthy and unrefined oils have a low smoke point and they become unhealthy under the heat in deep fryers. It is better to save them for salad dressings and cook your food with minimum oil.

Researches have hypothesized that eating too much "bad" oil can lead to increased inflammation in the body. What is worse, bad oils increase the amount of harmful LDL cholesterol in the bloodstream and speed up aging. Even small amounts of trans-fats can increase the risk of heart disease by 23%.

As for the Air Fryers, spritz non-stick oil all over ingredients in the cooking basket. You will end up with a perfect crunchy bite and moist interiors without submerging food in hot oil. As for the type of oil, connoisseurs recommend grapeseed, avocado, and light olive oil; they all have a high smoke point and neutral flavor. Sesame oil, with its rich and unique flavor, might be great for savory meals, but it is not a good choice for making a dessert. Avoid corn oil, palm oil, and soybean oil at all costs; these oils are partially hydrogenated, genetically modified and loaded with trans-fats. Margarine and fake butter alternatives should be avoided as well.

With this in mind, the Air Fryer will inspire you to cook healthy and well-balanced meals for your family.

Fast cooking. Cooking times in the Air Fryer are shorter in comparison with standard convection oven or convection toaster oven. Your Air Fryer heats up in a few minutes, then, hot air circulates quickly, cooking your food evenly on all sides. It can take about 50 minutes to roast chicken in a conventional oven; in an Air Fryer, it gets perfectly cooked, beautifully browned with crispy edges in 30 to 35 minutes. Many Air Fryer models come with dividers so that you can cook different dishes at the same time. The Air Fryer is a real winner for one-pot meals too. This is a space, cost, and frustration saving solution!

Convenience. The convenience and ease of use are one of the best features of your Air Fryer. With a user-friendly design, a simple touch operation and an "on/off" switch, an Air Fryer can be a great choice. In fact, cooking specifications are preprogrammed in advance and all you have to do is to push a button and go about your business. This intelligent machine will do the rest. If you often forget about food when it's cooking, an Air Fryer will give you peace of mind since it has a digital countdown timer and buzzer. In addition, the heat is maintained throughout the cooking time, eliminating the need to set cooking temperatures and watch over frying pans. On the other hand, you can stay in control of the cooking process since temperatures can be adjusted at any time and your device can be turned OFF at any time too.

Another convenience is that an Air Fryer won't smoke up your kitchen. Food baskets can easily be cleaned in a dishwasher. You can also use a sponge and a mild dishwashing soap. Besides being convenient, air fryers are safe to use.

More flavor. These fried foods do not taste like fat. These fried foods are really delicious! Extraordinary chips are only the beginning. Old-fashioned casseroles, spicy chilies, perfect mac and cheese, sophisticated appetizers, ooey-gooey bread puddings and delicious snacks turn out great in the Air Fryer.

All these advantages, make your Air Fryer a great choice when it comes to healthy dieting that does not compromise convenience and flavor.

Air Fryer Cooking Guide

CHICKEN	Temperature	Time (minutes)		Temperature	Time (minutes)
Breasts, bone in	370°F	20-25	Nuggets	390°F	6-10
Chicken wings	360°F	15-20	Whole chicken	360°F	70-75
Game Hen	390°F	20-22	Tenders	360°F	8-10
Legs	370°F	20-22	Thighs, boneless	380°F	18-20
Legs, bone in	380°F	28-30	Thighs, bone in	380°F	20-22

BEEF

	Temperature	Time (minutes)		Temperature	Time (minutes)
Burger	370°F	16-20	Meatballs (big)	380°F	10-12
Filet mignon	400°F	18	Ribeye	400°F	10-15
Flank steak	400°F	12-15	Round roast	390°F	45-55
London broil	400°F	20-28	Sirloin steaks	400°F	9-15
Meatballs (1-inch)	380°F	7-10			

PORK and LAMB

	Temperature	Time (minutes)		Temperature	Time (minutes)
Bacon	400°F	5-7	Rack of lamb	380°F	22
Bacon (thick cut)	400°F	6-10	Sausages	380°F	12-15
Lamb loin chops	400°F	6-10	Spare ribs	400°F	18-25
Loin	360°F	50-55	Tenderloin	400°F	5-8
Pork chops	400°F	12-15			

FISH

	Temperature	Time (minutes)		Temperature	Time (minutes)
Calamari	400°F	4-5	Swordfish steak	400°F	10-12
Fish sticks	390°F	6-10	Tuna steak	400°F	8-10
Fish fillet	400°F	10-12	Scallops	400°F	5-7
Salmon (fillet)	380°F	12	Shrimp	400°F	5-6
Shellfish	400°F	12-15			

VEGETABLES

	Temperature	Time (minutes)		Temperature	Time (minutes)
Asparagus	400°F	5-7	Mushrooms	400°F	5
Beets	400°F	40	Onions	400°F	8-10
Broccoli	400°F	6	Parsnip	380°F	15
Brussels Sprouts	380°F	15	Peppers	400°F	15
Carrots	380°F	13-15	Potatoes	400°F	12
Cauliflower	400°F	12-15	Potatoes (baby)	400°F	15
Corn on the cob	390°F	6-10	Squash	400°F	12-15
Eggplant	400°F	15	Sweet potato	380°F	35
Fennel	370°F	15	Tomato (cherry)	380°F	20-22
Green beans	400°F	5-7	Tomato	350°F	10
Kale	250°F	12	Zucchini	400°F	10

FROZEN FOOD

	Temperature	Time (minutes)		Temperature	Time (minutes)
Breaded shrimp	400°F	10-12	Mozzarella stick	400°F	8-10
Fish fillets	400°F	14-20	Onion rings	400°F	8
Fish sticks	400°F	10-12	Pot stickers	400°F	8-10
French fries (thin)	400°F	15-20			

POULTRY

Pretzel Crusted Chicken with Spicy Mustard Sauce

(Ready in about 20 minutes | Servings 6)

Per serving: 357 Calories; 17.6g Fat; 20.3g Carbs; 28.1g Protein; 2.8g Sugars

Ingredients

2 eggs

1 ½ pound chicken breasts, boneless, skinless, cut into bite-sized chunks

1/2 cup crushed pretzels

1 teaspoon shallot powder

1 teaspoon paprika

Sea salt and ground black pepper, to taste

1/2 cup vegetable broth

1 tablespoon cornstarch

3 tablespoons Worcestershire sauce

3 tablespoons tomato paste

1 tablespoon apple cider vinegar

2 tablespoons olive oil

2 garlic cloves, chopped

1 jalapeno pepper, minced

1 teaspoon yellow mustard

Directions

Start by preheating your Air Fryer to 390 degrees F.

In a mixing dish, whisk the eggs until frothy; toss the chicken chunks into the whisked eggs and coat well.

In another dish, combine the crushed pretzels with shallot powder, paprika, salt and pepper. Then, lay the chicken chunks in the pretzel mixture; turn it over until well coated.

Place the chicken pieces in the air fryer basket. Cook the chicken for 12 minutes, shaking the basket halfway through.

Meanwhile, whisk the vegetable broth with cornstarch, Worcestershire sauce, tomato paste, and apple cider vinegar.

Preheat a cast-iron skillet over medium flame. Heat the olive oil and sauté the garlic with jalapeno pepper for 30 to 40 seconds, stirring frequently.

Add the cornstarch mixture and let it simmer until the sauce has thickened a little. Now, add the air-fried chicken and mustard; let it simmer for 2 minutes more or until heated through.

Serve immediately and enjoy!

Chinese-Style Sticky Turkey Thighs

(Ready in about 35 minutes | Servings 6)

Per serving: 279 Calories; 10.1g Fat; 19g Carbs; 27.7g Protein; 17.9g Sugars

Ingredients

1 tablespoon sesame oil

2 pounds turkey thighs

1 teaspoon Chinese Five-spice powder

1 teaspoon pink Himalayan salt

1/4 teaspoon Sichuan pepper

6 tablespoons honey

1 tablespoon Chinese rice vinegar

2 tablespoons soy sauce

1 tablespoon sweet chili sauce

1 tablespoon mustard

Directions

Preheat your Air Fryer to 360 degrees F.

Brush the sesame oil all over the turkey thighs. Season them with spices.

Cook for 23 minutes, turning over once or twice. Make sure to work in batches to ensure even cooking

In the meantime, combine the remaining ingredients in a wok (or similar type pan) that is preheated over medium-high heat. Cook and stir until the sauce reduces by about a third.

Add the fried turkey thighs to the wok; gently stir to coat with the sauce.

Let the turkey rest for 10 minutes before slicing and serving. Enjoy!

Easy Hot Chicken Drumsticks

(Ready in about 40 minutes | Servings 6)

Per serving: 280 Calories; 18.7g Fat; 2.6g Carbs; 24.1g Protein; 1.4g Sugars

Ingredients

6 chicken drumsticks
Sauce:
6 ounces hot sauce
3 tablespoons olive oil
3 tablespoons tamari sauce
1 teaspoon dried thyme
1/2 teaspoon dried oregano

Directions

Spritz the sides and bottom of the cooking basket with a nonstick cooking spray.

Cook the chicken drumsticks at 380 degrees F for 35 minutes, flipping them over halfway through.

Meanwhile, heat the hot sauce, olive oil, tamari sauce, thyme, and oregano in a pan over medium-low heat; reserve.

Drizzle the sauce over the prepared chicken drumsticks; toss to coat well and serve. Bon appétit!

Crunchy Munchy Chicken Tenders with Peanuts

(Ready in about 25 minutes | Servings 4)

Per serving: 343 Calories; 16.4g Fat; 10.6g Carbs; 36.8g Protein; 1g Sugars

Ingredients

1 ½ pounds chicken tenderloins
2 tablespoons peanut oil
1/2 cup tortilla chips, crushed
Sea salt and ground black pepper, to taste
1/2 teaspoon garlic powder
1 teaspoon red pepper flakes
2 tablespoons peanuts, roasted and roughly chopped

Directions

Start by preheating your Air Fryer to 360 degrees F.

Brush the chicken tenderloins with peanut oil on all sides.

In a mixing bowl, thoroughly combine the crushed chips, salt, black pepper, garlic powder, and red pepper flakes. Dredge the chicken in the breading, shaking off any residual coating.

Lay the chicken tenderloins into the cooking basket. Cook for 12 to 13 minutes or until it is no longer pink in the center. Work in batches; an instant-read thermometer should read at least 165 degrees F.

Serve garnished with roasted peanuts. Bon appétit!

Tarragon Turkey Tenderloins with Baby Potatoes

(Ready in about 50 minutes | Servings 6)
Per serving: 317 Calories; 7.4g Fat; 14.2g Carbs; 45.7g Protein; 1.1g Sugars

Ingredients

2 pounds turkey tenderloins
2 teaspoons olive oil
Salt and ground black pepper, to taste
1 teaspoon smoked paprika
2 tablespoons dry white wine
1 tablespoon fresh tarragon leaves, chopped
1 pound baby potatoes, rubbed

Directions

Brush the turkey tenderloins with olive oil. Season with salt, black pepper, and paprika. Afterwards, add the white wine and tarragon.

Cook the turkey tenderloins at 350 degrees F for 30 minutes, flipping them over halfway through. Let them rest for 5 to 9 minutes before slicing and serving.

After that, spritz the sides and bottom of the cooking basket with the remaining 1 teaspoon of olive oil.

Then, preheat your Air Fryer to 400 degrees F; cook the baby potatoes for 15 minutes. Serve with the turkey and enjoy!

Mediterranean Chicken Breasts with Roasted Tomatoes

(Ready in about 1 hour | Servings 8)
Per serving: 315 Calories; 17.1g Fat; 2.7g Carbs; 36g Protein; 1.7g Sugars

Ingredients

2 teaspoons olive oil, melted
3 pounds chicken breasts, bone-in
1/2 teaspoon black pepper, freshly ground
1/2 teaspoon salt
1 teaspoon cayenne pepper
2 tablespoons fresh parsley, minced
1 teaspoon fresh basil, minced
1 teaspoon fresh rosemary, minced
4 medium-sized Roma tomatoes, halved

Directions

Start by preheating your Air Fryer to 370 degrees F. Brush the cooking basket with 1 teaspoon of olive oil.

Sprinkle the chicken breasts with all seasonings listed above.

Cook for 25 minutes or until chicken breasts are slightly browned. Work in batches.

Arrange the tomatoes in the cooking basket and brush them with the remaining teaspoon of olive oil. Season with sea salt.

Cook the tomatoes at 350 degrees F for 10 minutes, shaking halfway through the cooking time. Serve with chicken breasts. Bon appétit!

Thai Red Duck with Candy Onion

(Ready in about 25 minutes | Servings 4)
Per serving: 362 Calories; 18.7g Fat; 4g Carbs; 42.3g Protein; 1.3g Sugars

Ingredients

1 ½ pounds duck breasts, skin removed
1 teaspoon kosher salt
1/2 teaspoon cayenne pepper
1/3 teaspoon black pepper
1/2 teaspoon smoked paprika
1 tablespoon Thai red curry paste
1 cup candy onions, halved
1/4 small pack coriander, chopped

Directions

Place the duck breasts between 2 sheets of foil; then, use a rolling pin to bash the duck until they are 1-inch thick.

Preheat your Air Fryer to 395 degrees F.

Rub the duck breasts with salt, cayenne pepper, black pepper, paprika, and red curry paste. Place the duck breast in the cooking basket.

Cook for 11 to 12 minutes. Top with candy onions and cook for another 10 to 11 minutes. Serve garnished with coriander and enjoy!

Rustic Chicken Legs with Turnip Chips

(Ready in about 30 minutes | Servings 3)

Per serving: 207 Calories; 7.8g Fat; 3.4g Carbs; 29.5g Protein; 1.6g Sugars

Ingredients

1 pound chicken legs

1 teaspoon Himalayan salt

1 teaspoon paprika

1/2 teaspoon ground black pepper

1 teaspoon butter, melted

1 turnip, trimmed and sliced

Directions

Spritz the sides and bottom of the cooking basket with a nonstick cooking spray.

Season the chicken legs with salt, paprika, and ground black pepper.

Cook at 370 degrees F for 10 minutes. Increase the temperature to 380 degrees F.

Drizzle turnip slices with melted butter and transfer them to the cooking basket with the chicken. Cook the turnips and chicken for 15 minutes more, flipping them halfway through the cooking time.

As for the chicken, an instant-read thermometer should read at least 165 degrees F.

Serve and enjoy!

Old-Fashioned Chicken Drumettes

(Ready in about 30 minutes | Servings 3)

Per serving: 347 Calories; 9.1g Fat; 11.3g Carbs; 41g Protein; 0.1g Sugars

Ingredients

1/3 cup all-purpose flour

1/2 teaspoon ground white pepper

1 teaspoon seasoning salt

1 teaspoon garlic paste

1 teaspoon rosemary

1 whole egg + 1 egg white

6 chicken drumettes

1 heaping tablespoon fresh chives, chopped

Directions

Start by preheating your Air Fryer to 390 degrees. Mix the flour with white pepper, salt, garlic paste, and rosemary in a small-sized bowl.

In another bowl, beat the eggs until frothy.

Dip the chicken into the flour mixture, then into the beaten eggs; coat with the flour mixture one more time.

Cook the chicken drumettes for 22 minutes. Serve warm, garnished with chives.

Easy Ritzy Chicken Nuggets

(Ready in about 20 minutes | Servings 4)

Per serving: 355 Calories; 20.1g Fat; 5.3g Carbs; 36.6g Protein; 0.2g Sugars

Ingredients

1 ½ pounds chicken tenderloins, cut into small pieces

1/2 teaspoon garlic salt

1/2 teaspoon cayenne pepper

1/4 teaspoon black pepper, freshly cracked

4 tablespoons olive oil

1/3 cup saltines (e.g. Ritz crackers), crushed

4 tablespoons Parmesan cheese, freshly grated

Directions

Start by preheating your Air Fryer to 390 degrees F.

Season each piece of the chicken with garlic salt, cayenne pepper, and black pepper.

In a mixing bowl, thoroughly combine the olive oil with crushed saltines. Dip each piece of chicken in the cracker mixture.

Finally, roll the chicken pieces over the Parmesan cheese. Cook for 8 minutes, working in batches.

Later, if you want to warm the chicken nuggets, add them to the basket and cook for 1 minute more. Serve with French fries, if desired.

Asian Chicken Filets with Cheese

(Ready in about 50 minutes | Servings 2)

Per serving: 376 Calories; 19.6g Fat; 12.1g Carbs; 36.2g Protein; 3.4g Sugars

Ingredients

4 rashers smoked bacon

2 chicken filets

1/2 teaspoon coarse sea salt

1/4 teaspoon black pepper, preferably freshly ground

1 teaspoon garlic, minced

1 (2-inch) piece ginger, peeled and minced

1 teaspoon black mustard seeds

1 teaspoon mild curry powder

1/2 cup coconut milk

1/3 cup tortilla chips, crushed

1/2 cup Pecorino Romano cheese, freshly grated

Directions

Start by preheating your Air Fryer to 400 degrees F. Add the smoked bacon and cook in the preheated Air Fryer for 5 to 7 minutes. Reserve.

In a mixing bowl, place the chicken fillets, salt, black pepper, garlic, ginger, mustard seeds, curry powder, and milk. Let it marinate in your refrigerator about 30 minutes.

In another bowl, mix the crushed chips and grated Pecorino Romano cheese.

Dredge the chicken fillets through the chips mixture and transfer them to the cooking basket. Reduce the temperature to 380 degrees F and cook the chicken for 6 minutes.

Turn them over and cook for a further 6 minutes. Repeat the process until you have run out of ingredients.

Serve with reserved bacon. Enjoy!

Paprika Chicken Legs with Brussels Sprouts

(Ready in about 30 minutes | Servings 2)

Per serving: 355 Calories; 20.1g Fat; 5.3g Carbs; 36.6g Protein; 0.2g Sugars

Ingredients

2 chicken legs

1/2 teaspoon paprika

1/2 teaspoon kosher salt

1/2 teaspoon black pepper

1 pound Brussels sprouts

1 teaspoon dill, fresh or dried

Directions

Start by preheating your Air Fryer to 370 degrees F.

Now, season your chicken with paprika, salt, and pepper. Transfer the chicken legs to the cooking basket. Cook for 10 minutes.

Flip the chicken legs and cook an additional 10 minutes. Reserve.

Add the Brussels sprouts to the cooking basket; sprinkle with dill. Cook at 380 degrees F for 15 minutes, shaking the basket halfway through.

Serve with the reserved chicken legs. Bon appétit!

Chinese Duck (Xiang Su Ya)

(Ready in about 30 minutes + marinating time | Servings 6)

Per serving: 403 Calories; 25.3g Fat; 16.4g Carbs; 27.5g Protein; 13.2g Sugars

Ingredients

2 pounds duck breast, boneless
2 green onions, chopped
1 tablespoon light soy sauce
1 teaspoon Chinese 5-spice powder
1 teaspoon Szechuan peppercorns
3 tablespoons Shaoxing rice wine
1 teaspoon coarse salt
1/2 teaspoon ground black pepper
Glaze:
1/4 cup molasses
3 tablespoons orange juice
1 tablespoon soy sauce

Directions

In a ceramic bowl, place the duck breasts, green onions, light soy sauce, Chinese 5-spice powder, Szechuan peppercorns, and Shaoxing rice wine. Let it marinate for 1 hour in your refrigerator.

Preheat your Air Fryer to 400 degrees F for 5 minutes.

Now, discard the marinade and season the duck breasts with salt and pepper. Cook the duck breasts for 12 to 15 minutes or until they are golden brown. Repeat with the other ingredients. In the meantime, add the reserved marinade to the saucepan that is preheated over medium-high heat. Add the molasses, orange juice, and 1 tablespoon of soy sauce.

Bring to a simmer and then, whisk constantly until it gets syrupy. Brush the surface of duck breasts with glaze so they are completely covered. Place duck breasts back in the Air Fryer basket; cook an additional 5 minutes. Enjoy!

Turkey Bacon with Scrambled Eggs

(Ready in about 25 minutes | Servings 4)

Per serving: 456 Calories; 38.3g Fat; 6.3g Carbs; 21.4g Protein; 4.5g Sugars

Ingredients

1/2 pound turkey bacon
4 eggs
1/3 cup milk
2 tablespoons yogurt
1/2 teaspoon sea salt
1 bell pepper, finely chopped
2 green onions, finely chopped
1/2 cup Colby cheese, shredded

Directions

Place the turkey bacon in the cooking basket. Cook at 360 degrees F for 9 to 11 minutes. Work in batches. Reserve the fried bacon.

In a mixing bowl, thoroughly whisk the eggs with milk and yogurt. Add salt, bell pepper, and green onions.

Brush the sides and bottom of the baking pan with the reserved 1 teaspoon of bacon grease.

Pour the egg mixture into the baking pan. Cook at 355 degrees F about 5 minutes. Top with shredded Colby cheese and cook for 5 to 6 minutes more.

Serve the scrambled eggs with the reserved bacon and enjoy!

Italian Chicken and Cheese Frittata

(Ready in about 25 minutes | Servings 4)

Per serving: 329 Calories; 25.3g Fat; 3.4g Carbs; 21.1g Protein; 2.3g Sugars

Ingredients

1 (1-pound) fillet chicken breast
Sea salt and ground black pepper, to taste
1 tablespoon olive oil
4 eggs
1/2 teaspoon cayenne pepper
1/2 cup Mascarpone cream
1/4 cup Asiago cheese, freshly grated

Directions

Flatten the chicken breast with a meat mallet. Season with salt and pepper.

Heat the olive oil in a frying pan over medium flame. Cook the chicken for 10 to 12 minutes; slice into small strips, and reserve.

Then, in a mixing bowl, thoroughly combine the eggs, and cayenne pepper; season with salt to taste. Add the cheese and stir to combine.

Add the reserved chicken. Then, pour the mixture into a lightly greased pan; put the pan into the cooking basket.

Cook in the preheated Air Fryer at 355 degrees F for 10 minutes, flipping over halfway through.

Summer Meatballs with Cheese

(Ready in about 15 minutes | Servings 4)

Per serving: 497 Calories; 24g Fat; 20.7g Carbs; 41.9g Protein; 4.1g Sugars

Ingredients

1 pound ground turkey
1/2 pound ground pork
1 egg, well beaten
1 cup seasoned breadcrumbs
1 teaspoon dried basil
1 teaspoon dried rosemary
1/4 cup Manchego cheese, grated
2 tablespoons yellow onions, finely chopped
1 teaspoon fresh garlic, finely chopped
Sea salt and ground black pepper, to taste

Directions

In a mixing bowl, combine all the ingredients until everything is well incorporated.

Shape the mixture into 1-inch balls.

Cook the meatballs in the preheated Air Fryer at 380 degrees for 7 minutes. Shake halfway through the cooking time. Work in batches.

Serve with your favorite pasta. Bon appétit!

Dijon Roasted Sausage and Carrots

(Ready in about 20 minutes | Servings 3)

Per serving: 313 Calories; 13.6g Fat; 14.7g Carbs; 32.3g Protein; 7.2g Sugars

Ingredients

1 pound chicken sausages, smoked
1 pound carrots, trimmed and halved lengthwise
1 tablespoon Dijon mustard
2 tablespoons olive oil
1/2 teaspoon sea salt
1/4 teaspoon ground black pepper

Directions

Start by preheating your Air Fryer to 380 degrees F. Pierce the sausages all over with a fork and add them to the cooking basket.

Add the carrots and the remaining ingredients; toss until well coated.

Cook for 10 minutes in the preheated Air Fryer. Shake the basket and cook an additional 5 to 7 minutes. Serve warm.

Ranch Parmesan Chicken Wings

(Ready in about 25 minutes | Servings 3)

Per serving: 521 Calories; 34.2g Fat; 17.3g Carbs; 33.7g Protein; 1.4g Sugars

Ingredients

1/2 cup seasoned breadcrumbs

2 tablespoons butter, melted

6 tablespoons parmesan cheese, preferably freshly grated

1 tablespoon Ranch seasoning mix

2 tablespoons oyster sauce

6 chicken wings, bone-in

Directions

Start by preheating your Air Fryer to 370 degrees F.

In a resealable bag, place the breadcrumbs, butter, parmesan, Ranch seasoning mix, and oyster sauce. Add the chicken wings and shake to coat on all sides.

Arrange the chicken wings in the Air Fryer basket. Spritz the chicken wings with a nonstick cooking spray.

Cook for 11 minutes. Turn them over and cook an additional 11 minutes. Serve warm with your favorite dipping sauce, if desired. Enjoy!

Lemon-Basil Turkey Breast

(Ready in about 1 hour | Servings 4)

Per serving: 416 Calories; 22.6g Fat; 0g Carbs; 49g Protein; 0g Sugars

Ingredients

2 tablespoons olive oil

2 pounds turkey breasts, bone-in skin-on

Coarse sea salt and ground black pepper, to taste

1 teaspoon fresh basil leaves, chopped

2 tablespoons lemon zest, grated

Directions

Rub olive oil on all sides of the turkey breasts; sprinkle with salt, pepper, basil, and lemon zest. Place the turkey breasts skin side up on a parchment-lined cooking basket.

Cook in the preheated Air Fryer at 330 degrees F for 30 minutes. Now, turn them over and cook an additional 28 minutes.

Serve with lemon wedges, if desired. Bon appétit!

Agave Mustard Glazed Chicken

(Ready in about 30 minutes | Servings 4)

Per serving: 471 Calories; 24.6g Fat; 13.1g Carbs; 47.4g Protein; 12.7g Sugars

Ingredients

1 tablespoon avocado oil

2 pounds chicken breasts, boneless, skin-on

1 tablespoon Jamaican Jerk Rub

1/2 teaspoon salt

3 tablespoons agave syrup

1 tablespoon mustard

2 tablespoons scallions, chopped

Directions

Start by preheating your Air Fryer to 370 degrees F.

Drizzle the avocado oil all over the chicken breast. Then, rub the chicken breast with the Jamaican Jerk rub.

Cook in the preheated Air Fryer approximately 15 minutes. Turn them over and cook an additional 8 minutes.

While the chicken breasts are roasting, combine the salt, agave syrup, and mustard in a pan over medium heat. Let it simmer until the glaze thickens.

After that, brush the glaze all over the chicken breast. Air-fry for a further 6 minutes or until the surface is crispy. Serve garnished with fresh scallions. Bon appétit!

Thanksgiving Turkey Tenderloin with Gravy

(Ready in about 40 minutes | Servings 4)

Per serving: 374 Calories; 8.1g Fat; 20.5g Carbs; 52g Protein; 10.2g Sugars

Ingredients

2 ½ pounds turkey tenderloin, sliced into pieces

1/2 head of garlic, peeled and halved

1 dried marjoram

Sea salt and ground black pepper, to taste

1 teaspoon cayenne pepper

Gravy:

3 cups vegetable broth

1/3 cup all-purpose flour

Sea salt and ground black pepper, to taste

Directions

Start by preheating your Air Fryer to 350 degrees F.

Rub the turkey tenderloins with garlic halves; add marjoram, salt, black pepper, and cayenne pepper.

Cook the turkey tenderloins at 350 degrees F for 30 minutes or until an instant-read thermometer inserted into the center of the breast reaches 165 degrees F; flip them over halfway through.

In a saucepan, place the drippings from the roasted turkey. Add 1 cup of broth and 1/6 cup of flour to the pan; whisk until it makes a smooth paste.

Once it gets a golden brown color, add the rest of the chicken broth and flour. Sprinkle with salt and pepper to taste.

Let it simmer over medium heat, stirring constantly for 6 to 7 minutes. Serve with warm turkey tenderloin and enjoy!

Roasted Citrus Turkey Drumsticks

(Ready in about 55 minutes | Servings 3)

Per serving: 352 Calories; 23.4g Fat; 5.2g Carbs; 29.3g Protein; 2.6g Sugars

Ingredients

3 medium turkey drumsticks, bone-in skin-on

1/2 butter stick, melted

Sea salt and ground black pepper, to taste

1 teaspoon cayenne pepper

1 teaspoon fresh garlic, minced

1 teaspoon dried parsley flakes

1 teaspoon onion powder

Zest of one orange

1/4 cup orange juice

Directions

Rub all ingredients onto the turkey drumsticks.

Preheat your Air Fryer to 400 degrees F. Cook the turkey drumsticks for 16 minutes in the preheated Air Fryer.

Loosely cover with foil and cook an additional 24 minutes.

Once cooked, let it rest for 10 minutes before slicing and serving. Bon appétit!

Garden Vegetable and Chicken Casserole

(Ready in about 30 minutes | Servings 4)

Per serving: 333 Calories; 10.7g Fat; 5.4g Carbs; 50g Protein; 1.2g Sugars

Ingredients

2 teaspoons peanut oil

2 pounds chicken drumettes

1 garlic clove, minced

1/2 medium-sized leek, sliced

2 carrots, sliced

1 cup cauliflower florets

1 tablespoon all-purpose flour

2 cups vegetable broth

1/4 cup dry white wine

1 thyme sprig

1 rosemary sprig

Directions

Preheat your Air Fryer to 370 degrees F. Then, drizzle the chicken drumettes with peanut oil and cook them for 10 minutes. Transfer the chicken drumettes to a lightly greased pan.

Add the garlic, leeks, carrots, and cauliflower.

Mix the remaining ingredients in a bowl. Pour the flour mixture into the pan. Cook at 380 degrees F for 15 minutes.

Serve warm.

Creole Turkey with Peppers

(Ready in about 35 minutes | Servings 4)

Per serving: 426 Calories; 15.4g Fat; 12.4g Carbs; 51g Protein; 6.1g Sugars

Ingredients

2 pounds turkey thighs, skinless and boneless

1 red onion, sliced

2 bell peppers, deveined and sliced

1 habanero pepper, deveined and minced

1 carrot, sliced

1 tablespoon Creole seasoning mix

1 tablespoon fish sauce

2 cups chicken broth

Directions

Preheat your Air Fryer to 360 degrees F. Now, spritz the bottom and sides of the casserole dish with a nonstick cooking spray.

Arrange the turkey thighs in the casserole dish. Add the onion, pepper, and carrot. Sprinkle with Creole seasoning.

Afterwards, add the fish sauce and chicken broth. Cook in the preheated Air Fryer for 30 minutes. Serve warm and enjoy!

PORK

Rustic Pizza with Ground Pork

(Ready in about 30 minutes | Servings 4)

Per serving: 529 Calories; 9.6g Fat; 65.5g Carbs; 37.9g Protein; 0.9g Sugars

Ingredients

1 (10-count) can refrigerator biscuits

4 tablespoons tomato paste

1 tablespoon tomato ketchup

2 teaspoons brown mustard

1/2 cup ground pork

1/2 cup ground beef sausage

1 red onion, thinly sliced

1/2 cup mozzarella cheese, shredded

Directions

Spritz the sides and bottom of a baking pan with a nonstick cooking spray.

Press five biscuits into the pan. Brush the top of biscuit with 2 tablespoons of tomato paste.

Add 1/2 tablespoon of ketchup, 1 teaspoon of mustard, 1/4 cup of ground pork, 1/4 cup of beef sausage. Top with 1/2 of the red onion slices.

Bake in the preheated Air Fryer at 360 degrees F for 10 minutes. Top with 1/4 cup of mozzarella cheese and bake another 5 minutes.

Repeat the process with the second pizza. Slice the pizza into halves, serve and enjoy!

Pork Koftas with Yoghurt Sauce

(Ready in about 25 minutes | Servings 4)

Per serving: 407 Calories; 28.5g Fat; 3.4g Carbs; 32.9g Protein; 1.3g Sugars

Ingredients

2 teaspoons olive oil

1/2 pound ground pork

1/2 pound ground beef

1 egg, whisked

Sea salt and ground black pepper, to taste

1 teaspoon paprika

2 garlic cloves, minced

1 teaspoon dried marjoram

1 teaspoon mustard seeds

1/2 teaspoon celery seeds

Yogurt Sauce:

2 tablespoons olive oil

2 tablespoons fresh lemon juice

Sea salt, to taste

1/4 teaspoon red pepper flakes, crushed

1/2 cup full-fat yogurt

1 teaspoon dried dill weed

Directions

Spritz the sides and bottom of the cooking basket with 2 teaspoons of olive oil.

In a mixing dish, thoroughly combine the ground pork, beef, egg, salt, black pepper, paprika, garlic, marjoram, mustard seeds, and celery seeds.

Form the mixture into kebabs and transfer them to the greased cooking basket. Cook at 365 degrees F for 11 to 12 minutes, turning them over once or twice.

In the meantime, mix all the sauce ingredients and place in the refrigerator until ready to serve. Serve the pork koftas with the yogurt sauce on the side. Enjoy!

Spicy Bacon-Wrapped Tater Tots

(Ready in about 25 minutes | Servings 5)

Per serving: 297 Calories; 26.1g Fat; 9.3g Carbs; 7.1g Protein; 3.2g Sugars

Ingredients

10 thin slices of bacon

10 tater tots, frozen

1 teaspoon cayenne pepper

Sauce:

1/4 cup mayo

4 tablespoons ketchup

1 teaspoon rice vinegar

1 teaspoon chili powder

Directions

Lay the slices of bacon on your working surface. Place a tater tot on one end of each slice; sprinkle with cayenne pepper and roll them over.

Cook in the preheated Air Fryer at 390 degrees F for 15 to 16 minutes.

Whisk all ingredients for the sauce in a mixing bowl and store in your refrigerator, covered, until ready to serve.

Serve Bacon-Wrapped Tater Tots with the sauce on the side. Enjoy!

Pork Cutlets with a Twist

(Ready in about 1 hour 20 minutes | Servings 2)

Per serving: 579 Calories; 19.4g Fat; 50g Carbs; 49.6g Protein; 2.2g Sugars

Ingredients

1 cup water

1 cup red wine

1 tablespoon sea salt

2 pork cutlets

1/2 cup all-purpose flour

1 teaspoon shallot powder

1/2 teaspoon porcini powder

Sea salt and ground black pepper, to taste

1 egg

1/4 cup yogurt

1 teaspoon brown mustard

1 cup tortilla chips, crushed

Directions

In a large ceramic dish, combine the water, wine and salt. Add the pork cutlets and put for 1 hour in the refrigerator.

In a shallow bowl, mix the flour, shallot powder, porcini powder, salt, and ground pepper. In another bowl, whisk the eggs with yogurt and mustard.

In a third bowl, place the crushed tortilla chips.

Dip the pork cutlets in the flour mixture and toss evenly; then, in the egg mixture. Finally, roll them over the crushed tortilla chips.

Spritz the bottom of the cooking basket with cooking oil. Add the breaded pork cutlets and cook at 395 degrees F and for 10 minutes.

Flip and cook for 5 minutes more on the other side. Serve warm.

Cheesy Creamy Pork Casserole

(Ready in about 25 minutes | Servings 4)

Per serving: 433 Calories; 20.4g Fat; 2.6g Carbs; 56.5g Protein; 0.3g Sugars

Ingredients

2 tablespoons olive oil

2 pounds pork tenderloin, cut into serving-size pieces

1 teaspoon coarse sea salt

1/2 teaspoon freshly ground pepper

1/4 teaspoon chili powder

1 teaspoon dried marjoram

1 tablespoon mustard

1 cup Ricotta cheese

1 ½ cups chicken broth

Directions

Start by preheating your Air Fryer to 350 degrees F.

Heat the olive oil in a pan over medium-high heat. Once hot, cook the pork for 6 to 7 minutes, flipping it to ensure even cooking.

Arrange the pork in a lightly greased casserole dish. Season with salt, black pepper, chili powder, and marjoram.

In a mixing dish, thoroughly combine the mustard, cheese, and chicken broth. Pour the mixture over the pork chops in the casserole dish. Bake for another 15 minutes or until bubbly and heated through. Bon appétit!

Herbed Pork Loin with Carrot Chips

(Ready in about 1 hour 15 minutes | Servings 4)
Per serving: 461 Calories; 25.8g Fat; 10.8g Carbs; 44g Protein; 5.3g Sugars

Ingredients

1 tablespoon peanut oil

1 ½ pounds pork loin, cut into 4 pieces

Coarse sea salt and ground black pepper, to taste

1/2 teaspoon onion powder

1 teaspoon garlic powder

1/2 teaspoon cayenne pepper

1/2 teaspoon dried rosemary

1/2 teaspoon dried basil

1/2 teaspoon dried oregano

1 pound carrots, cut into matchsticks

1 tablespoon coconut oil, melted

Directions

Drizzle 1 tablespoon of peanut oil all over the pork loin. Season with salt, black pepper, onion powder, garlic powder, cayenne pepper, rosemary, basil, and oregano.

Cook in the preheated Air Fryer at 360 degrees F for 55 minutes; make sure to turn the pork over every 15 minutes to ensure even cooking.

Test for doneness with a meat thermometer.

Toss the carrots with melted coconut oil; season to taste and cook in the preheated Air Fryer at 380 degrees F for 15 minutes.

Serve the warm pork loin with the carrots on the side. Enjoy!

Easy Pork & Parmesan Meatballs

(Ready in about 15 minutes | Servings 3)
Per serving: 539 Calories; 38.4g Fat; 17.5g Carbs; 29.2g Protein; 4.3g Sugars

Ingredients

1 pound ground pork

2 tablespoons tamari sauce

1 teaspoon garlic, minced

2 tablespoons spring onions, finely chopped

1 tablespoon brown sugar

1 tablespoon olive oil

1/2 cup breadcrumbs

2 tablespoons parmesan cheese, preferably freshly grated

Directions

Combine the ground pork, tamari sauce, garlic, onions, and sugar in a mixing dish. Mix until everything is well incorporated.

Form the mixture into small meatballs.

In a shallow bowl, mix the olive oil, breadcrumbs, and parmesan. Roll the meatballs over the parmesan mixture.

Cook at 380 degrees F for 3 minutes; shake the basket and cook an additional 4 minutes or until meatballs are browned on all sides. Bon appétit!

Italian-Style Honey Roasted Pork

(Ready in about 50 minutes | Servings 3)

Per serving: 314 Calories; 9.8g Fat; 13g Carbs; 41.8g Protein; 11.8g Sugars

Ingredients

1 teaspoon Celtic sea salt

1/2 teaspoon black pepper, freshly cracked

1/4 cup red wine

2 tablespoons mustard

2 tablespoons honey

2 garlic cloves, minced

1 pound pork top loin

1 tablespoon Italian herb seasoning blend

Directions

In a ceramic bowl, mix the salt, black pepper, red wine, mustard, honey, and garlic. Add the pork top loin and let it marinate at least 30 minutes.

Spritz the sides and bottom of the cooking basket with a nonstick cooking spray.

Place the pork top loin in the basket; sprinkle with the Italian herb seasoning blend.

Cook the pork tenderloin at 370 degrees F for 10 minutes. Flip halfway through, spraying with cooking oil and cook for 5 to 6 minutes more. Serve immediately.

Ground Pork and Cheese Casserole

(Ready in about 45 minutes | Servings 4)

Per serving: 561 Calories; 28g Fat; 22.2g Carbs; 52.5g Protein; 7.7g Sugars

Ingredients

1 tablespoon olive oil

1 ½ pounds pork, ground

Sea salt and ground black pepper, to taste

1 medium-sized leek, sliced

1 teaspoon fresh garlic, minced

2 carrots, trimmed and sliced

1 (2-ounce) jar pimiento, drained and chopped

1 can (10 ¾-ounces) condensed cream of mushroom soup

1 cup water

1/2 cup ale

1 cup cream cheese

1/2 cup soft fresh breadcrumbs

1 tablespoon fresh cilantro, chopped

Directions

Start by preheating your Air Fryer to 320 degrees F.

Add the olive oil to a baking dish and heat for 1 to 2 minutes. Add the pork, salt, pepper and cook for 6 minutes, crumbling with a fork.

Add the leeks and cook for 4 to 5 minutes, stirring occasionally.

Add the garlic, carrots, pimiento, mushroom soup, water, ale, and cream cheese. Gently stir to combine.

Turn the temperature to 370 degrees F.

Top with the breadcrumbs. Place the baking dish in the cooking basket and cook approximately 30 minutes or until everything is thoroughly cooked. Serve garnished with fresh cilantro. Bon appétit!

Mexican-Style Ground Pork with Peppers

(Ready in about 40 minutes | Servings 4)

Per serving: 505 Calories; 39.4g Fat; 9.9g Carbs; 28g Protein; 5.1g Sugars

Ingredients

2 chili peppers

1 red bell pepper

2 tablespoons olive oil

1 large-sized shallot, chopped

1 pound ground pork

2 garlic cloves, minced

2 ripe tomatoes, pureed

1 teaspoon dried marjoram

1/2 teaspoon mustard seeds

1/2 teaspoon celery seeds

1 teaspoon Mexican oregano

1 tablespoon fish sauce

2 tablespoons fresh coriander, chopped

Salt and ground black pepper, to taste

2 cups water

1 tablespoon chicken bouillon granules

2 tablespoons sherry wine

1 cup Mexican cheese blend

Directions

Roast the peppers in the preheated Air Fryer at 395 degrees F for 10 minutes, flipping them halfway through cook time.

Let them steam for 10 minutes; then, peel the skin and discard the stems and seeds. Slice the peppers into halves.

Heat the olive oil in a baking pan at 380 degrees F for 2 minutes; add the shallots and cook for 4 minutes. Add the ground pork and garlic; cook for a further 4 to 5 minutes.

After that, stir in the tomatoes, marjoram, mustard seeds, celery seeds, oregano, fish sauce, coriander, salt, and pepper. Add a layer of sliced peppers to the baking pan.

Mix the water with the chicken bouillon granules and sherry wine. Add the mixture to the baking pan.

Cook in the preheated Air Fryer at 395 degrees F for 10 minutes. Top with cheese and bake an additional 5 minutes until the cheese has melted. Serve immediately.

Pork Shoulder with Molasses Sauce

(Ready in about 25 minutes + marinating time | Servings 3)

Per serving: 353 Calories; 19.6g Fat; 13.5g Carbs; 29.2g Protein; 12.2g Sugars

Ingredients

2 tablespoons molasses

2 tablespoons soy sauce

2 tablespoons Shaoxing wine

2 garlic cloves, minced

1 teaspoon fresh ginger, minced

1 tablespoon cilantro stems and leaves, finely chopped

1 pound boneless pork shoulder

2 tablespoons sesame oil

Directions

In a large-sized ceramic dish, thoroughly combine the molasses, soy sauce, wine, garlic, ginger, and cilantro; add the pork shoulder and allow it to marinate for 2 hours in the refrigerator. Then, grease the cooking basket with sesame oil. Place the pork shoulder in the cooking basket; reserve the marinade.

Cook in the preheated Air Fryer at 395 degrees F for 14 to 17 minutes, flipping and basting with the marinade halfway through. Let it rest for 5 to 6 minutes before slicing and serving.

While the pork is roasting, cook the marinade in a preheated skillet over medium heat; cook until it has thickened.

Brush the pork shoulder with the sauce and enjoy!

Tender Spare Ribs

(Ready in about 35 minutes + marinating time | Servings 4)

Per serving: 443 Calories; 35.2g Fat; 10g Carbs; 20.5g Protein; 3.1g Sugars

Ingredients

1 rack pork spareribs, fat trimmed and cut in half

2 tablespoons fajita seasoning

2 tablespoons smoked paprika

Sea salt and pepper, to taste

1 tablespoon prepared brown mustard

3 tablespoons Worcestershire sauce

1/2 cup beer

1 tablespoon peanut oil

Directions

Toss the spareribs with the fajita seasoning, paprika, salt, pepper, mustard, and Worcestershire sauce. Pour in the beer and let it marinate for 1 hour in your refrigerator.

Rub the sides and bottom of the cooking basket with peanut oil.

Cook the spareribs in the preheated Air Fryer at 365 degrees for 17 minutes. Turn the ribs over and cook an additional 14 to 15 minutes. Serve warm. Bon appétit!

Pork Belly with New Potatoes

(Ready in about 50 minutes | Servings 4)

Per serving: 547 Calories; 30.2g Fat; 20.9g Carbs; 45.1g Protein; 1.1g Sugars

Ingredients

1 ½ pounds pork belly, cut into 4 pieces

Kosher salt and ground black pepper, to taste

1 teaspoon smoked paprika

1/2 teaspoon turmeric powder

2 tablespoons oyster sauce

2 tablespoons green onions

4 cloves garlic, sliced

1 pound new potatoes, scrubbed

Directions

Preheat your Air Fryer to 390 degrees F. Pat dry the pork belly and season with all spices listed above.

Add the oyster sauce and spritz with a nonstick cooking spray on all sides. Now, cook in the preheated Air Fryer for 30 minutes. Turn them over every 10 minutes.

Increase the temperature to 400 degrees F. Add the green onions, garlic, and new potatoes.

Cook another 15 minutes, shaking occasionally. Serve warm.

Smoky Mini Meatloaves with Cheese

(Ready in about 50 minutes | Servings 4)

Per serving: 585 Calories; 38.4g Fat; 22.2g Carbs; 38.5g Protein; 14.6g Sugars

Ingredients

1 pound ground pork

1/2 pound ground beef

1 package onion soup mix

1/2 cup seasoned bread crumbs

4 tablespoons Romano cheese, grated

2 eggs

1 carrot, grated

1 bell pepper, chopped

1 serrano pepper, minced

2 scallions, chopped

2 cloves garlic, finely chopped

2 tablespoons soy sauce sauce

Sea salt and black pepper, to your liking

Glaze:

1/2 cup tomato paste

2 tablespoons ketchup

1 tablespoon brown mustard

1 teaspoon smoked paprika

1 tablespoon honey

Directions

In a large mixing bowl, thoroughly combine all ingredients for the meatloaf. Mix with your hands until everything is well incorporated.

Then, shape the mixture into four mini loaves. Transfer them to the cooking basket previously generously greased with cooking oil.

Cook in the preheated Air Fryer at 385 degrees F approximately 43 minutes.

Mix all ingredients for the glaze. Spread the glaze over mini meatloaves and cook for another 6 minutes. Bon appétit!

Asian Sticky Ribs

(Ready in about 40 minutes | Servings 4)

Per serving: 446 Calories; 29.6g Fat; 5.5g Carbs; 45.1g Protein; 4.1g Sugars

Ingredients

1 teaspoon salt

1 teaspoon cayenne pepper

1/2 teaspoon ground black pepper

2 teaspoons raw honey

2 garlic cloves, minced

1 (1-inch) piece ginger, peeled and grated

1/2 teaspoon onion powder

1/2 teaspoon porcini powder

1 teaspoon mustard seeds

1 tablespoon sweet chili sauce

1 tablespoon balsamic vinegar

1 ½ pounds pork country-style ribs

Directions

In a mixing bowl, combine the salt, cayenne pepper, black pepper, honey, garlic, ginger, onion powder, porcini powder, mustard seeds, sweet chili sauce, and balsamic vinegar.

Toss and rub the seasoning mixture all over the pork ribs.

Cook the country-style ribs at 360 degrees F for 15 minutes; flip the ribs and cook an additional 20 minutes or until they are tender inside and crisp on the outside.

Serve warm, garnished with fresh chives if desired.

Smoked Sausage with Sauerkraut

(Ready in about 35 minutes | Servings 4)

Per serving: 478 Calories; 42.6g Fat; 6.1g Carbs; 17.2g Protein; 2.1g Sugars

Ingredients

4 pork sausages, smoked

2 tablespoons canola oil

2 garlic cloves, minced

1 pound sauerkraut

1 teaspoon cayenne pepper

1/2 teaspoon black peppercorns

2 bay leaves

Directions

Start by preheating your Air Fryer to 360 degrees F.

Prick holes into the sausages using a fork and transfer them to the cooking basket. Cook approximately 14 minutes, shaking the basket a couple of times. Set aside.

Now, heat the canola oil in a baking pan at 380 degrees F. Add the garlic and cook for 1 minute. Immediately stir in the sauerkraut, cayenne pepper, peppercorns, and bay leaves.

Let it cook for 15 minutes, stirring every 5 minutes. Serve in individual bowls with warm sausages on the side!

Boston Butt with Salsa Verde

(Ready in about 35 minutes | Servings 4)

Per serving: 374 Calories; 24.1g Fat; 8.6g Carbs; 29.9g Protein; 4.7g Sugars

Ingredients

1 pound Boston butt, thinly sliced across the grain into 2-inch-long strips

1/2 teaspoon red pepper flakes, crushed

Sea salt and ground black pepper, to taste

1/2 pound tomatillos, chopped

1 small-sized onion, chopped

2 chili peppers, chopped

2 cloves garlic

2 tablespoons fresh cilantro, chopped

1 tablespoon olive oil

1 teaspoon sea salt

Directions

Rub the Boston butt with red pepper, salt, and black pepper. Spritz the bottom of the cooking basket with a nonstick cooking spray.

Roast the Boston butt in the preheated Air Fryer at 390 degrees F for 10 minutes. Shake the basket and cook another 10 minutes.

While the pork is roasting, make the salsa.

Blend the remaining ingredients until smooth and uniform. Transfer the mixture to a saucepan and add 1 cup of water.

Bring to a boil; reduce the heat and simmer for 8 to 12 minutes. Serve the roasted pork with the salsa verde on the side. Enjoy!

Blade Steaks with Butter-Fried Broccoli

(Ready in about 30 minutes | Servings 4)

Per serving: 443 Calories; 29.5g Fat; 11.3g Carbs; 34.2g Protein; 2.8g Sugars

Ingredients

1 ½ pounds blade steaks skinless, boneless

Kosher salt and ground black pepper, to taste

2 garlic cloves, crushed

2 tablespoons soy sauce

1 tablespoon oyster sauce

2 tablespoon lemon juice

1 pound broccoli, broken into florets

2 tablespoons butter, melted

1 teaspoon dried dill weed

2 tablespoons sunflower seeds, lightly toasted

Directions

Start by preheating your Air Fryer to 385 degrees F. Spritz the bottom and sides of the cooking basket with cooking spray.

Now, season the pork with salt and black pepper. Add the garlic, soy sauce, oyster sauce, and lemon juice.

Cook for 20 minutes; turning over halfway through the cooking time.

Toss the broccoli with the melted butter and dill. Add the broccoli to the cooking basket and cook at 400 degrees F for 6 minutes, shaking the basket periodically.

Serve the warm pork with broccoli and garnish with sunflower seeds. Bon appétit!

Authentic Spaghetti Bolognese

(Ready in about 30 minutes | Servings 4)

Per serving: 551 Calories; 25.9g Fat; 50.1g Carbs; 29.1g Protein; 5.5g Sugars

Ingredients

2 tablespoons olive oil

1 shallot, peeled and chopped

1 teaspoon fresh garlic, minced

1 pound lean ground pork

1 cup tomato puree

2 tablespoons apple cider vinegar

1 teaspoon oregano

1 teaspoon basil

1 teaspoon rosemary

Salt and black pepper, to taste

1 package spaghetti

1 tablespoon fresh parsley

Directions

Heat the oil in a baking pan at 380 degrees F. Then, sauté the shallots until tender about 4 minutes.

Add the garlic and ground pork; cook an additional 6 minutes, stirring and crumbling meat with a spatula.

Add the tomato puree, vinegar, and spices; cook for 4 to 6 minutes longer or until everything is heated through.

Meanwhile, bring a large pot of lightly salted water to a boil. Cook your spaghetti for 10 to 12 minutes; drain and divide between individual plates.

Top with the Bolognese sauce and serve garnished with fresh parsley. Bon appétit!

Perfect Sloppy Joes

(Ready in about 30 minutes | Servings 4)

Per serving: 545 Calories; 32g Fat; 38.1g Carbs; 26.1g Protein; 3.9g Sugars

Ingredients

1 tablespoon olive oil

1 shallot, chopped

2 garlic cloves, minced

1 bell pepper, chopped

1 pound ground pork

2 ripe medium-sized tomatoes, pureed

1 tablespoon Worcestershire sauce

1 tablespoon poultry seasoning blend

Dash ground allspice

6 hamburger buns

Directions

Start by preheating your Air Fryer to 390 degrees F. Heat the olive oil for a few minutes.

Once hot, sauté the shallots until just tender. Add the garlic and bell pepper; cook for 4 minutes more or until they are aromatic.

Add the ground pork and cook for 5 minutes more, crumbling with a fork. Next step, stir in the pureed tomatoes, Worcestershire sauce, and spices. Decrease the temperature to 365 degrees F and cook another 10 minutes.

Spoon the meat mixture into hamburger buns and transfer them to the cooking basket. Cook for 7 minutes or until thoroughly warmed.

Easy Pork Sandwiches

(Ready in about 55 minutes | Servings 3)

Per serving: 453 Calories; 8.9g Fat; 33.4g Carbs; 56.8g Protein; 11.6g Sugars

Ingredients

2 teaspoons peanut oil

1 ½ pounds pork sirloin

Coarse sea salt and ground black pepper, to taste

1 tablespoon smoked paprika

1/4 cup prepared barbecue sauce

3 hamburger buns, split

Directions

Start by preheating your Air Fryer to 360 degrees F.

Drizzle the oil all over the pork sirloin. Sprinkle with salt, black pepper, and paprika.

Cook for 50 minutes in the preheated Air Fryer. Remove the roast from the Air Fryer and shred with two forks. Mix in the barbecue sauce. Serve over hamburger buns. Enjoy!

Egg Noodles with Sausage-Pepper Sauce

(Ready in about 30 minutes | Servings 4)

Per serving: 389 Calories; 32.2g Fat; 11.4g Carbs; 13.6g Protein; 5.7g Sugars

Ingredients

1 tablespoon lard, at room temperature

2 garlic cloves, smashed

2 scallions, chopped

1 red bell pepper, chopped

1 green bell pepper, chopped

1 pound pork sausages, sliced

2 ripe tomatoes, pureed

2 tablespoons tomato ketchup

1 teaspoon molasses

1 tablespoon flax seed meal

Salt and black pepper, to taste

1 teaspoon basil

1 teaspoon rosemary

1 teaspoon oregano

1 package egg noodles

Directions

Melt the lard in a baking pan at 380 degrees F. Once hot, sauté the garlic, scallions, and peppers until tender about 2 minutes.

Add the sausages and cook an additional 5 minutes, stirring occasionally.

Add the tomato puree, tomato ketchup, molasses, flax seed meal, and spices; cook for 4 to 5 minutes more or until everything is thoroughly warmed and the sauce has thickened.

Meanwhile, bring a large pot of lightly salted water to a boil. Cook the egg noodles for 10 to 12 minutes; drain and divide between individual plates. Top with the warm sauce and serve. Bon appétit!

Sticky Dijon Pork Chops

(Ready in about 20 minutes | Servings 4)

Per serving: 307 Calories; 14g Fat; 8.3g Carbs; 33.9g Protein; 7.1g Sugars

Ingredients

1/4 cup soy sauce

2 tablespoons brown sugar

1/4 cup rice vinegar

1 pound pork loin center rib chops, bone-in

Celtic salt and ground black pepper, to taste

1 tablespoon Dijon mustard

Directions

Thoroughly combine the soy sauce, brown sugar, and vinegar; add the pork and let it marinate for 1 hour in the refrigerator.

Sprinkle the pork chops with salt and black pepper. Spread the mustard, all over the pork chops.

Cook in the preheated Air Fryer at 400 degrees F for 12 minutes. Serve warm with mashed potatoes if desired.

Pork Loin with Mushroom Sauce

(Ready in about 30 minutes | Servings 4)

Per serving: 416 Calories; 13.9g Fat; 15.2g Carbs; 55.1g Protein; 4.4g Sugars

Ingredients

2 pounds top loin, boneless

1 tablespoon olive oil

1 teaspoon Celtic salt

1/4 teaspoon ground black pepper, or more to taste

2 shallots, sliced

2 garlic cloves, minced

1 cup mushrooms, chopped

2 tablespoons all-purpose flour

3/4 cup cream of mushroom soup

1 teaspoon chili powder

Salt, to taste

Directions

Pat dry the pork and drizzle with olive oil. Season with Celtic salt and pepper. Cook in the preheated Air Fryer at 370 degrees F for 10 minutes.

Top with shallot slices and cook another 10 minutes.

Test the temperature of the meat; it should be around 150 degrees F. Reserve the pork and onion, keeping warm.

Add the cooking juices to a saucepan and preheat over medium-high heat. Cook the garlic and mushrooms until aromatic about 2 minutes.

Combine the flour with the mushroom soup. Add the flour mixture to the pan along with the chili powder and salt. Gradually stir into the pan. Bring to a boil; immediately turn the heat to medium and cook for 2 to 3 minutes stirring frequently. Spoon the sauce over the reserved pork and onion. Enjoy!

Sausage and Mushroom Chili

(Ready in about 35 minutes | Servings 4)

Per serving: 569 Calories; 35.3g Fat; 33.1g Carbs; 33.1g Protein; 10.4g Sugars

Ingredients

1 tablespoon olive oil

1 shallot, chopped

2 garlic cloves, smashed

10 ounces button mushrooms, sliced

1/2 pound pork sausages, chopped

2 cups tomato puree

2 tablespoons tomato ketchup

1 teaspoon yellow mustard

1 cup chicken broth

2 teaspoons ancho chili powder

Salt and ground black pepper, to taste

1 (16-ounce) can pinto beans, rinsed and drained

1/2 cup cream cheese

Directions

Start by preheating your Air Fryer to 360 degrees F. Heat the oil in a baking pan for a few minutes and cook the shallot until tender about 4 minutes. Add the garlic and mushrooms; cook another 4 minutes or until tender and fragrant.

Next, stir in sausage and cook for a further 9 minutes. Add tomato puree, ketchup, mustard, and broth. Stir to combine and cook another 6 minutes.

Add spices and beans; cook an additional 7 minutes. Divide between individual bowls and top each bowl with cream cheese. Enjoy!

Easy Keto Pork Rinds

(Ready in about 30 minutes | Servings 10)

Per serving: 470 Calories; 48g Fat; 0.1g Carbs; 8.4g Protein; 0g Sugars

Ingredients

2 pounds pork belly, trim the fat layer and cut into cubes

1 teaspoon Celtic salt

1 tablespoon red pepper flakes, crushed

Directions

Add the pork, salt, and red pepper to the baking pan. Bake at 395 degrees F for 10 minutes.

Pat it dry and transfer to your refrigerator to cool for 15 minutes.

Process the pork fat in the blender until it resembles coarse breadcrumbs. Use with your favorite keto creations!

StLouis-Style Pork Ribs with Roasted Peppers

(Ready in about 55 minutes | Servings 2)

Per serving: 444 Calories; 25.4g Fat; 10g Carbs; 43.3g Protein; 4.9g Sugars

2 pounds St. Louis-style pork spareribs, individually cut

1 teaspoon seasoned salt

1/2 teaspoon ground black pepper

1 tablespoon sweet paprika

1/2 teaspoon mustard powder

2 tablespoons sesame oil

4 bell pepper, seeded

Directions

Toss and rub the spices all over the pork ribs; drizzle with 1 tablespoon of sesame oil.

Cook the pork ribs at 360 degrees F for 15 minutes; flip the ribs and cook an additional 20 minutes or until they are tender inside and crisp on the outside.

Toss the peppers with the remaining 1 tablespoon of oil; season to taste and cook in the preheated Air Fryer at 390 degrees F for 15 minutes.

Serve the warm spareribs with the roasted peppers on the side. Enjoy!

BEEF

Dijon Top Chuck with Herbs

(Ready in about 1 hour | Servings 3)

Per serving: 406 Calories; 24.1g Fat; 0.3g Carbs; 44.1g Protein; 0g Sugars

Ingredients

1 ½ pounds top chuck

2 teaspoons olive oil

1 tablespoon Dijon mustard

Sea salt and ground black pepper, to taste

1 teaspoon dried marjoram

1 teaspoon dried thyme

1/2 teaspoon fennel seeds

Directions

Start by preheating your Air Fryer to 380 degrees F

Add all ingredients in a Ziploc bag; shake to mix well. Next, spritz the bottom of the Air Fryer basket with cooking spray.

Place the beef in the cooking basket and cook for 50 minutes, turning every 10 to 15 minutes.

Let it rest for 5 to 7 minutes before slicing and serving. Enjoy!

Mediterranean-Style Beef Steak and Zucchini

(Ready in about 20 minutes | Servings 4)

Per serving: 396 Calories; 20.4g Fat; 3.5g Carbs; 47.8g Protein; 0.1g Sugars

Ingredients

1 ½ pounds beef steak

1 pound zucchini

1 teaspoon dried rosemary

1 teaspoon dried basil

1 teaspoon dried oregano

2 tablespoons extra-virgin olive oil

2 tablespoons fresh chives, chopped

Directions

Start by preheating your Air Fryer to 400 degrees F.

Toss the steak and zucchini with the spices and olive oil. Transfer to the cooking basket and cook for 6 minutes.

Now, shale the basket and cook another 6 minutes. Serve immediately garnished with fresh chives. Enjoy!

Peperonata with Beef Sausage

(Ready in about 35 minutes | Servings 4)

Per serving: 563 Calories; 41.5g Fat; 10.6g Carbs; 35.6g Protein; 7.9g Sugars

Ingredients

2 teaspoons canola oil

2 bell peppers, sliced

1 green bell pepper, sliced

1 serrano pepper, sliced

1 shallot, sliced

Sea salt and pepper, to taste

1/2 dried thyme

1 teaspoon dried rosemary

1/2 teaspoon mustard seeds

1 teaspoon fennel seeds

2 pounds thin beef parboiled sausage

Directions

Brush the sides and bottom of the cooking basket with 1 teaspoon of canola oil. Add the peppers and shallot to the cooking basket.

Toss them with the spices and cook at 390 degrees F for 15 minutes, shaking the basket occasionally. Reserve.

Turn the temperature to 380 degrees F

Then, add the remaining 1 teaspoon of oil. Once hot, add the sausage and cook in the preheated Air Frye for 15 minutes, flipping them halfway through the cooking time.

Serve with reserved pepper mixture. Bon appétit!

New York Strip with Mustard Butter

(Ready in about 20 minutes | Servings 4)

Per serving: 459 Calories; 27.4g Fat; 2.5g Carbs; 48.3g Protein; 1.4g Sugars

Ingredients

1 tablespoon peanut oil

2 pounds New York Strip

1 teaspoon cayenne pepper

Sea salt and freshly cracked black pepper, to taste

1/2 stick butter, softened

1 teaspoon whole-grain mustard

1/2 teaspoon honey

Directions

Rub the peanut oil all over the steak; season with cayenne pepper, salt, and black pepper.

Cook in the preheated Air Fryer at 400 degrees F for 7 minutes; turn over and cook an additional 7 minutes.

Meanwhile, prepare the mustard butter by whisking the butter, whole-grain mustard, and honey.

Serve the roasted New York Strip dolloped with the mustard butter. Bon appétit!

Scotch Fillet with Sweet 'n' Sticky Sauce

(Ready in about 40 minutes | Servings 4)

Per serving: 556 Calories; 17.9g Fat; 25.8g Carbs; 60g Protein; 10.4g Sugars

Ingredients

2 pounds scotch fillet, sliced into strips

4 tablespoons tortilla chips, crushed

2 green onions, chopped

Sauce:

1 tablespoon butter

2 garlic cloves, minced

1/2 teaspoon dried rosemary

1/2 teaspoon dried dill

1/2 cup beef broth

1 tablespoons fish sauce

2 tablespoons honey

Directions

Start by preheating your Air Fryer to 390 degrees F.

Coat the beef strips with the crushed tortilla chips on all sides. Spritz with cooking spray on all sides and transfer them to the cooking basket. Cook for 30 minutes, shaking the basket every 10 minutes.

Meanwhile, heat the sauce ingredient in a saucepan over medium-high heat. Bring to a boil and reduce the heat; cook until the sauce has thickened slightly.

Add the steak to the sauce; let it sit approximately 8 minutes. Serve over the hot egg noodles if desired.

Roasted Ribeye with Garlic Mayo

(Ready in about 20 minutes | Servings 3)

Per serving: 437 Calories; 24.8g Fat; 1.8g Carbs; 51g Protein; 0.1g Sugars

Ingredients

1 ½ pounds ribeye, bone-in

1 tablespoon butter, room temperature

Salt, to taste

1/2 teaspoon crushed black pepper

1/2 teaspoon dried dill

1/2 teaspoon cayenne pepper

1/2 teaspoon garlic powder

1/2 teaspoon onion powder

1 teaspoon ground coriander

3 tablespoons mayonnaise

1 teaspoon garlic, minced

Directions

Start by preheating your Air Fryer to 400 degrees F.

Pat dry the ribeye and rub it with softened butter on all sides. Sprinkle with seasonings and transfer to the cooking basket.

Cook in the preheated Air Fryer for 15 minutes, flipping them halfway through the cooking time. In the meantime, simply mix the mayonnaise with garlic and place in the refrigerator until ready to serve. Bon appétit!

Crustless Beef and Cheese Tart

(Ready in about 25 minutes | Servings 4)

Per serving: 572 Calories; 44.6g Fat; 16.2g Carbs; 28.1g Protein; 8.9g Sugars

Ingredients

1 tablespoon canola oil

1 onion, finely chopped

2 fresh garlic cloves, minced

1/2 pound ground chuck

1/2 pound Chorizo sausage, crumbled

1 cup pasta sauce

Sea salt, to taste

1/4 teaspoon ground black pepper

1/2 teaspoon red pepper flakes, crushed

1 cup cream cheese, room temperature

1/2 cup Swiss cheese, shredded

1 egg

1/2 cup crackers, crushed

Directions

Start by preheating your Air Fryer to 370 degrees F.

Grease a baking pan with canola oil.

Add the onion, garlic, ground chuck, sausage, pasta sauce, salt, black pepper, and red pepper. Cook for 9 minutes.

In the meantime, combine cheese with egg. Place the cheese-egg mixture over the beef mixture. Sprinkle with crushed crackers and cook for 10 minutes. Serve warm and enjoy!

Beef Taco Roll-Ups with Cotija Cheese

(Ready in about 25 minutes | Servings 4)

Per serving: 417 Calories; 15.9g Fat; 41g Carbs; 26.2g Protein; 1.5g Sugars

Ingredients

1 tablespoon sesame oil

2 tablespoons scallions, chopped

1 garlic clove, minced

1 bell pepper, chopped

1/2 pound ground beef

1/2 teaspoon Mexican oregano

1/2 teaspoon dried marjoram

1 teaspoon chili powder

1/2 cup refried beans

Sea salt and ground black pepper, to taste

1/2 cup Cotija cheese, shredded

8 roll wrappers

Directions

Start by preheating your Air Fryer to 395 degrees F.

Heat the sesame oil in a nonstick skillet over medium-high heat. Cook the scallions, garlic, and peppers until tender and fragrant.

Add the ground beef, oregano, marjoram, and chili powder. Continue cooking for 3 minutes longer or until it is browned.

Stir in the beans, salt, and pepper. Divide the meat/bean mixture between wrappers that are softened with a little bit of water. Top with cheese.

Roll the wrappers and spritz them with cooking oil on all sides.

Cook in the preheated Air Fryer for 11 to 12 minutes, flipping them halfway through the cooking time. Enjoy!

Barbecue Skirt Steak

(Ready in about 20 minutes + marinating time | Servings 5)

Per serving: 394 Calories; 19g Fat; 4.4g Carbs; 51.3g Protein; 3.3g Sugars

Ingredients

2 pounds skirt steak
2 tablespoons tomato paste
1 tablespoon tomato ketchup
1 tablespoon olive oil
1 tablespoon soy sauce
1/4 cup rice vinegar
1 tablespoon fish sauce
Sea salt, to taste
1/2 teaspoon dried dill
1/2 teaspoon dried rosemary
1/4 teaspoon black pepper, freshly cracked
1 tablespoon brown sugar

Directions

Place all ingredients in a large ceramic dish; let it marinate for 3 hours in your refrigerator.

Coat the sides and bottom of the Air Fryer with cooking spray.

Add your steak to the cooking basket; reserve the marinade. Cook the skirt steak in the preheated

Air Fryer at 400 degrees F for 12 minutes, turning over a couple of times, basting with the reserved marinade.

Serve warm with roasted new potatoes, if desired.

Meatballs with Cranberry Sauce

(Ready in about 40 minutes | Servings 4)

Per serving: 520 Calories; 22.4g Fat; 44g Carbs; 45.4g Protein; 25.5g Sugars

Ingredients

Meatballs:
1 ½ pounds ground chuck
1 egg
1 cup rolled oats
1/2 cup Romano cheese, grated
1/2 teaspoon dried basil
1/2 teaspoon dried oregano
1 teaspoon paprika
2 garlic cloves, minced
2 tablespoons scallions, chopped
Sea salt and cracked black pepper, to taste
Cranberry Sauce:
10 ounces BBQ sauce
8 ounces cranberry sauce

Directions

In a large bowl, mix all ingredients for the meatballs. Mix until everything is well incorporated; then, shape the meat mixture into 2-inch balls using a cookie scoop.

Transfer them to the lightly greased cooking basket and cook at 380 degrees F for 10 minutes. Shake the basket occasionally and work in batches.

Add the BBQ sauce and cranberry sauce to a saucepan and cook over moderate heat until you achieve a glaze-like consistency; it will take about 15 minutes.

Gently stir in the air fried meatballs and cook an additional 3 minutes or until heated through. Enjoy!

Kid-Friendly Mini Meatloaves

(Ready in about 30 minutes | Servings 4)

Per serving: 451 Calories; 27.6g Fat; 15.3g Carbs; 33.4g Protein; 3.7g Sugars

Ingredients

2 tablespoons bacon, chopped

1 small-sized onion, chopped

1 bell pepper, chopped

1 garlic clove, minced

1 pound ground beef

1/2 teaspoon dried basil

1/2 teaspoon dried mustard seeds

1/2 teaspoon dried marjoram

Salt and black pepper, to taste

1/2 cup panko crumbs

4 tablespoons tomato puree

Directions

Heat a nonstick skillet over medium-high heat; cook the bacon for 1 to 2 minutes; add the onion, bell pepper, and garlic and cook another 3 minutes or until fragrant.

Heat off. Stir in the ground beef, spices, and panko crumbs. Stir until well combined. Shape the mixture into four mini meatloaves.

Preheat your Air Fryer to 350 degrees F. Spritz the cooking basket with nonstick spray.

Place the mini meatloaves in the cooking basket and cook for 10 minutes; turn them over, top with the tomato puree and continue to cook for 10 minutes more. Bon appétit!

Quick Sausage and Veggie Sandwiches

(Ready in about 35 minutes | Servings 4)

Per serving: 627 Calories; 41.9g Fat; 41.3g Carbs; 22.2g Protein; 9.3g Sugars

Ingredients

4 bell peppers

2 tablespoons canola oil

4 medium-sized tomatoes, halved

4 spring onions

4 beef sausages

4 hot dog buns

1 tablespoon mustard

Directions

Start by preheating your Air Fryer to 400 degrees F.

Add the bell peppers to the cooking basket. Drizzle 1 tablespoon of canola oil all over the bell peppers.

Cook for 5 minutes. Turn the temperature down to 350 degrees F. Add the tomatoes and spring onions to the cooking basket and cook an additional 10 minutes.

Reserve your vegetables.

Then, add the sausages to the cooking basket. Drizzle with the remaining tablespoon of canola oil.

Cook in the preheated Air Fryer at 380 degrees F for 15 minutes, flipping them halfway through the cooking time.

Add the sausage to a hot dog bun; top with the air-fried vegetables and mustard; serve.

Mayonnaise and Rosemary Grilled Steak

(Ready in about 20 minutes | Servings 4)

Per serving: 620 Calories; 50g Fat; 2.8g Carbs; 39.7g Protein; 1.3g Sugars

Ingredients

1 cup mayonnaise

1 tablespoon fresh rosemary, finely chopped

2 tablespoons Worcestershire sauce

Sea salt, to taste

1/2 teaspoon ground black pepper

1 teaspoon smoked paprika

1 teaspoon garlic, minced

1 ½ pounds short loin steak

Directions

Combine the mayonnaise, rosemary, Worcestershire sauce, salt, pepper, paprika, and garlic; mix to combine well.

Now, brush the mayonnaise mixture over both sides of the steak. Lower the steak onto the grill pan.

Grill in the preheated Air Fryer at 390 degrees F for 8 minutes. Turn the steaks over and grill an additional 7 minutes.

Check for doneness with a meat thermometer. Serve warm and enjoy!

Cheesy Beef Burrito

(Ready in about 20 minutes | Servings 4)

Per serving: 468 Calories; 23.5g Fat; 22.1g Carbs; 42.7g Protein; 2.3g Sugars

Ingredients

1 pound rump steak

1 teaspoon garlic powder

1/2 teaspoon onion powder

1/2 teaspoon cayenne pepper

1 teaspoon piri piri powder

1 teaspoon Mexican oregano

Salt and ground black pepper, to taste

1 cup Mexican cheese blend

4 large whole wheat tortillas

1 cup iceberg lettuce, shredded

Directions

Toss the rump steak with the garlic powder, onion powder, cayenne pepper, piri piri powder, Mexican oregano, salt, and black pepper.

Cook in the preheated Air Fryer at 390 degrees F for 10 minutes. Slice against the grain into thin strips. Add the cheese blend and cook for 2 minutes more.

Spoon the beef mixture onto the wheat tortillas; top with lettuce; roll up burrito-style and serve.

Tender Marinated Flank Steak

(Ready in about 20 minutes + marinating time | Servings 4)

Per serving: 312 Calories; 15.5g Fat; 2.5g Carbs; 36.8g Protein; 1.9g Sugars

Ingredients

1 ½ pounds flank steak

1/2 cup red wine

1/2 cup apple cider vinegar

2 tablespoons soy sauce

Salt, to taste

1/2 teaspoon ground black pepper

1/2 teaspoon red pepper flakes, crushed

1/2 teaspoon dried basil

1 teaspoon thyme

Directions

Add all ingredients to a large ceramic bowl. Cover and let it marinate for 3 hours in your refrigerator.

Transfer the flank steak to the Air Fryer basket that is previously greased with nonstick cooking oil.

Cook in the preheated Air Fryer at 400 degrees F for 12 minutes, flipping over halfway through the cooking time. Bon appétit!

Korean-Style Breakfast Patties

(Ready in about 20 minutes | Servings 4)

Per serving: 377 Calories; 19.3g Fat; 2.4g Carbs; 45.9g Protein; 0.7g Sugars

Ingredients

1 ½ pounds ground beef

1 teaspoon garlic, minced

2 tablespoons scallions, chopped

Sea salt and cracked black pepper, to taste

1 teaspoon Gochugaru (Korean chili powder)

1/2 teaspoon dried marjoram

1 teaspoon dried thyme

1 teaspoon mustard seeds

1/2 teaspoon shallot powder

1/2 teaspoon cumin powder

1/2 teaspoon paprika

1 tablespoon liquid smoke flavoring

Directions

In a mixing bowl, thoroughly combine all ingredients until well combined.

Shape into four patties and spritz them with cooking oil on both sides. Bake at 357 degrees F for 18 minutes, flipping over halfway through the cooking time.

Serve on hamburger buns if desired. Bon appétit!

New York Strip with Pearl Onions

(Ready in about 20 minutes + marinating time | Servings 4)

Per serving: 445 Calories; 28g Fat; 11.2g Carbs; 36.6g Protein; 5.3g Sugars

Ingredients

1 ½ pounds New York strip, cut into strips

1 (1-pound) head cauliflower, broken into florets

1 cup pearl onion, sliced

Marinade:

1/4 cup tamari sauce

1 tablespoon olive oil

2 cloves garlic, minced

1 teaspoon of ground ginger

1/4 cup tomato paste

1/4 cup red wine

Directions

Mix all ingredients for the marinade. Add the beef to the marinade and let it sit in your refrigerator for 1 hour.

Preheat your Air Fryer to 400 degrees F. Transfer the meat to the Air Fryer basket. Add the cauliflower and onions.

Drizzle a few tablespoons of marinade all over the meat and vegetables. Cook for 12 minutes, shaking the basket halfway through the cooking time. Serve warm.

Beef and Vegetable Stir Fry

(Ready in about 35 minutes + marinating time | Servings 4)

Per serving: 418 Calories; 12.2g Fat; 4.8g Carbs; 68.2g Protein; 2.3g Sugars

Ingredients

2 pounds top round, cut into bite-sized strips

2 garlic cloves, sliced

1 teaspoon dried marjoram

1/4 cup red wine

1 tablespoon tamari sauce

Salt and black pepper, to taste

1 tablespoon olive oil

1 red onion, sliced

2 bell peppers, sliced

1 carrot, sliced

Directions

Place the top round, garlic, marjoram, red wine, tamari sauce, salt and pepper in a bowl, cover and let it marinate for 1 hour.

Preheat your Air Fryer to 390 degrees F and add the oil.

Once hot, discard the marinade and cook the beef for 15 minutes. Add the onion, peppers, carrot, and garlic and continue cooking until tender about 15 minutes more.

Open the Air Fryer every 5 minutes and baste the meat with the remaining marinade. Serve immediately.

Grilled London Broil with Mustard

(Ready in about 30 minutes + marinating time | Servings 4)

Per serving: 531 Calories; 24.1g Fat; 8.7g Carbs; 70g Protein; 6.2g Sugars

Ingredients

For the marinade:

2 tablespoons Worcestershire sauce

2 garlic cloves, minced

1 tablespoon oil

2 tablespoons rice vinegar

1 tablespoon molasses

London Broil:

2 pounds London broil

2 tablespoons tomato paste

Sea salt and cracked black pepper, to taste

1 tablespoon mustard

Directions

Combine all the marinade ingredients in a mixing bowl; add the London boil to the bowl. Cover and let it marinate for 3 hours.

Preheat the Air Fryer to 400 degrees F. Spritz the Air Fryer grill pan with cooking oil.

Grill the marinated London broil in the preheated Air Fryer for 18 minutes. Turn

London broil over, top with the tomato paste, salt, black pepper, and mustard.

Continue to grill an additional 10 minutes. Serve immediately.

Homemade Beef Empanadas

(Ready in about 35 minutes | Servings 5)

Per serving: 490 Calories; 35.1g Fat; 32g Carbs; 15.1g Protein; 13.2g Sugars

Ingredients

1 teaspoon olive oil

1/2 onion, chopped

1 garlic clove, minced

1/2 pound ground beef chuck

1 tablespoon raisins

1/2 teaspoon dried oregano

1/2 cup tomato paste

1/2 cup vegetable broth

Salt and ground pepper, to taste

10 Goya discs pastry dough

2 egg whites, beaten

Directions

Heat the oil in a saucepan over medium-high heat. Once hot, sauté the onion and garlic until tender, about 3 minutes.

Then, add the beef and continue to sauté an additional 4 minutes, crumbling with a fork.

Add the raisins, oregano, tomato paste, vegetable broth, salt, and black pepper. Reduce the heat to low and cook an additional 15 minutes.

Preheat the Air Fryer to 330 degrees F. Brush the Air Fryer basket with cooking oil. Divide the sauce between discs. Fold each of the discs in half and seal the edges. Brush the tops with the beaten eggs.

Bake for 7 to 8 minutes, working with batches. Serve with salsa sauce if desired. Enjoy!

Indonesian Beef with Peanut Sauce

(Ready in about 25 minutes + marinating time | Servings 4)

Per serving: 425 Calories; 20.1g Fat; 11.2g Carbs; 50g Protein; 7.9g Sugars

Ingredients

2 pounds filet mignon, sliced into bite-sized strips

1 tablespoon oyster sauce

2 tablespoons sesame oil

2 tablespoons tamari sauce

1 tablespoon ginger-garlic paste

1 tablespoon mustard

1 tablespoon honey

1 teaspoon chili powder

1/4 cup peanut butter

2 tablespoons lime juice

1 teaspoon red pepper flakes

2 tablespoons water

Directions

Place the beef strips, oyster sauce, sesame oil, tamari sauce, ginger-garlic paste, mustard, honey, and chili powder in a large ceramic dish.

Cover and allow it to marinate for 2 hours in your refrigerator.

Cook in the preheated Air Fryer at 400 degrees F for 18 minutes, shaking the basket occasionally.

Mix the peanut butter with lime juice, red pepper flakes, and water. Spoon the sauce onto the air fried beef strips and serve warm.

Beef Skewers with Pearl Onions and Eggplant

(Ready in about 1 hour 30 minutes | Servings 4)

Per serving: 500 Calories; 20.6g Fat; 12.8g Carbs; 63.3g Protein; 6.6g Sugars

Ingredients

1 ½ pounds beef stew meat cubes

1/4 cup mayonnaise

1/4 cup sour cream

1 tablespoon yellow mustard

1 tablespoon Worcestershire sauce

1 cup pearl onions

1 medium-sized eggplant, 1 ½-inch cubes

Sea salt and ground black pepper, to taste

Directions

In a mixing bowl, toss all ingredients until everything is well coated.

Place in your refrigerator, cover, and let it marinate for 1 hour.

Soak wooden skewers in water for 15 minutes

Thread the beef cubes, pearl onions and eggplant onto skewers. Cook in preheated Air Fryer at 395 degrees F for 12 minutes, flipping halfway through the cooking time. Serve warm.

Sunday Tender Skirt Steak

(Ready in about 20 minutes + marinating time | Servings 4)

Per serving: 503 Calories; 24.5g Fat; 21.7g Carbs; 46.2g Protein; 19.2g Sugars

Ingredient

1/3 cup soy sauce

4 tablespoon molasses

2 garlic cloves, minced

2 tablespoons champagne vinegar

1 teaspoon shallot powder

1 teaspoon porcini powder

1 teaspoon celery seeds

1 teaspoon paprika

1 ½ pounds skirt steak, cut into slices

Sea salt and ground black pepper, to taste

Directions

Place the soy sauce, molasses, garlic, vinegar, shallot powder, porcini powder, celery seeds, paprika, and beef in a large resealable plastic bag. Shake well and let it marinate overnight.

Discard the marinade and place the beef in the Air Fryer basket. Season with salt and black pepper to taste.

Cook in the preheated Air Fryer at 400 degrees F for 12 minutes, flipping and basting with the reserved marinade halfway through the cooking time. Bon appétit!

Beef with Creamed Mushroom Sauce

(Ready in about 20 minutes | Servings 5)
Per serving: 349 Calories; 16.2g Fat; 7.4g Carbs; 42.9g Protein; 2.6g Sugars

Ingredients

2 tablespoons butter
2 pounds sirloin, cut into four pieces
Salt and cracked black pepper, to taste
1 teaspoon cayenne pepper
1/2 teaspoon dried rosemary
1/2 teaspoon dried dill
1/4 teaspoon dried thyme
1 pound Cremini mushrooms, sliced
1 cup sour cream
1 teaspoon mustard
1/2 teaspoon curry powder

Directions

Start by preheating your Air Fryer to 396 degrees F. Grease a baking pan with butter.

Add the sirloin, salt, black pepper, cayenne pepper, rosemary, dill, and thyme to the baking pan. Cook for 9 minutes.

Next, stir in the mushrooms, sour cream, mustard, and curry powder. Continue to cook

another 5 minutes or until everything is heated through.

Spoon onto individual serving plates. Bon appétit!

Beef and Sausage Meatloaf with Peppers

(Ready in about 35 minutes | Servings 4)
Per serving: 415 Calories; 32.2g Fat; 4.4g Carbs; 25.3g Protein; 1.5g Sugars

Ingredients

1/2 pound beef sausage, crumbled
1/2 pound ground beef
1/4 cup pork rinds
2 tablespoons Parmesan, preferably freshly grated
1 shallot, finely chopped
2 garlic cloves, minced
Sea salt and ground black pepper, to taste
1 red bell pepper, finely chopped
1 serrano pepper, finely chopped

Directions

Start by preheating your Air Fryer to 390 degrees F.

Mix all ingredients in a bowl. Knead until everything is well incorporated.

Shape the mixture into a meatloaf and place in the baking pan that is previously greased with cooking oil.

Cook for 24 minutes in the preheated Air Fryer.

Let it stand on a cooling rack for 6 minutes before slicing and serving. Enjoy!

Burgers with Caramelized Onions

(Ready in about 30 minutes | Servings 4)
Per serving: 475 Calories; 21.1g Fat; 33.3g Carbs; 36.2g Protein; 6.1g Sugars

Ingredients

1 pound ground beef
Salt and ground black pepper, to taste
1 teaspoon garlic powder
1/2 teaspoon cumin powder
1 tablespoon butter
1 red onion, sliced
1 teaspoon brown sugar
1 tablespoon balsamic vinegar
1 tablespoon vegetable stock
4 hamburger buns
8 tomato slices
4 teaspoons mustard

Directions

Start by preheating your Air Fryer to 370 degrees F. Spritz the cooking basket with nonstick cooking oil.

Mix the ground beef with salt, pepper, garlic powder, and cumin powder. Shape the meat mixture into four patties and transfer them to the preheated Air Fryer.

Cook for 10 minutes; turn them over and cook on the other side for 8 to 10 minutes more.

While the burgers are frying, melt the butter in a pan over medium-high heat. Then, add the red onion and sauté for 4 minutes or until soft.

Add the brown sugar, vinegar, and stock and cook for 2 to 3 minute more.

To assemble your burgers, add the beef patties to the hamburger buns. Top with the caramelized onion, tomato, and mustard. Serve immediately and enjoy!

Authentic Dum Kebab with Raita Sauce

(Ready in about 25 minutes | Servings 4)
Per serving: 530 Calories; 31.1g Fat; 10.3g Carbs; 49.3g Protein; 6.1g Sugars

Ingredients

1 ½ pounds ground chuck
1 egg
1 medium-sized leek, chopped
2 garlic cloves, smashed
2 tablespoons fresh parsley, chopped
1 teaspoon fresh rosemary, chopped
Sea salt, to taste
1/2 teaspoon ground black pepper
1/2 teaspoon chili powder
1 teaspoon garam masala
1 teaspoon papaya paste
1 teaspoon ginger paste
1/2 teaspoon ground cumin
Raita Sauce:
1 small-sized cucumber, grated and squeezed
A pinch of salt
1 cup full-fat yogurt
1/4 cup fresh cilantro, coarsely chopped
1 tablespoon fresh lime juice

Directions

Combine all ingredients until everything is well incorporated. Press the meat mixture into a baking pan.

Cook in the preheated Air Fryer at 360 degrees F for 15 minutes. Taste for doneness with a meat thermometer.

Meanwhile, mix all ingredients for the sauce. Serve the warm meatloaf with the sauce on the side. Enjoy!

Moroccan-Style Steak Salad

(Ready in about 20 minutes | Servings 4)

Per serving: 522 Calories; 21.7g Fat; 28.2g Carbs; 51.3g Protein; 13.5g Sugars

Ingredients

2 pounds flank steak

1/4 cup soy sauce

4 tablespoons dry red wine

Salt, to taste

1/2 teaspoon ground black pepper

2 parsnips, peeled and sliced lengthways

1 teaspoon paprika

1 teaspoon onion powder

1 teaspoon garlic powder

1/2 teaspoon ground coriander

1/4 teaspoon ground allspice

2 tablespoons olive oil

2 tablespoons lime juice

1 teaspoon honey

1 cup lettuce leaves, shredded

1/2 cup pomegranate seeds

Directions

Place the flank steak, soy sauce, wine, salt, and black pepper in a ceramic bowl. Let it marinate for 2 hours in your refrigerator.

Transfer the meat to a lightly greased cooking basket. Top with parsnips. Add the paprika, onion powder, garlic powder, coriander, and allspice.

Cook in the preheated Air Fryer at 400 degrees F for 7 minutes; turn over and cook an additional 5 minutes.

In the meantime, make the dressing by mixing olive oil with lime juice and honey.

Put the lettuce leaves and roasted parsnip in a salad bowl; toss with the dressing. Slice the steaks and place on top of the salad. Sprinkle over the pomegranate seeds and serve. Enjoy!

FISH & SEAFOOD

Tuna Steaks with Pearl Onions

(Ready in about 20 minutes | Servings 4)

Per serving: 332 Calories; 5.9g Fat; 10.5g Carbs; 56.1g Protein; 6.1g Sugars

Ingredients

4 tuna steaks

1 pound pearl onions

4 teaspoons olive oil

1 teaspoon dried rosemary

1 teaspoon dried marjoram

1 tablespoon cayenne pepper

1/2 teaspoon sea salt

1/2 teaspoon black pepper, preferably freshly cracked

1 lemon, sliced

Directions

Place the tuna steaks in the lightly greased cooking basket. Top with the pearl onions; add the olive oil, rosemary, marjoram, cayenne pepper, salt, and black pepper.

Bake in the preheated Air Fryer at 400 degrees F for 9 to 10 minutes. Work in two batches.

Serve warm with lemon slices and enjoy!

Tortilla-Crusted Haddock Fillets

(Ready in about 20 minutes | Servings 2)

Per serving: 384 Calories; 21.3g Fat; 7.6g Carbs; 38.4g Protein; 1g Sugars

Ingredients

2 haddock fillets

1/2 cup tortilla chips, crushed

2 tablespoons parmesan cheese, freshly grated

1 teaspoon dried parsley flakes

1 egg, beaten

1/2 teaspoon coarse sea salt

1/4 teaspoon ground black pepper

1/4 teaspoon cayenne pepper

2 tablespoons olive oil

Directions

Start by preheating your Air Fryer to 360 degrees F. Pat dry the haddock fillets and set aside.

In a shallow bowl, thoroughly combine the crushed tortilla chips with the parmesan and parsley flakes. Mix until everything is well incorporated.

In a separate shallow bowl, whisk the egg with salt, black pepper, and cayenne pepper.

Dip the haddock fillets into the egg. Then, dip the fillets into the tortilla/parmesan mixture until well coated on all sides.

Drizzle the olive oil all over the fish fillets. Lower the coated fillets into the lightly greased Air Fryer basket. Cook for 11 to 13 minutes. Bon appétit!

Vermouth and Garlic Shrimp Skewers

(Ready in about 15 minutes + marinating time | Servings 4)

Per serving: 371 Calories; 12.2g Fat; 30.4g Carbs; 29.5g Protein; 3.2g Sugars

Ingredients

1 ½ pounds shrimp

1/4 cup vermouth

2 cloves garlic, crushed

1 teaspoon dry mango powder

Kosher salt, to taste

1/4 teaspoon black pepper, freshly ground

2 tablespoons olive oil

4 tablespoons flour

8 skewers, soaked in water for 30 minutes

1 lemon, cut into wedges

Directions

Add the shrimp, vermouth, garlic, mango powder, salt, black pepper, and olive oil in a ceramic bowl; let it sit for 1 hour in your refrigerator.

Discard the marinade and toss the shrimp with flour. Thread on to skewers and transfer to the lightly greased cooking basket.

Cook at 400 degrees F for 5 minutes, tossing halfway through. Serve with lemon wedges. Bon appétit!

Easy Lobster Tails

(Ready in about 20 minutes | Servings 5)

Per serving: 422 Calories; 7.9g Fat; 49.9g Carbs; 35.4g Protein; 3.1g Sugars

Ingredients

2 pounds fresh lobster tails, cleaned and halved, in shells

2 tablespoons butter, melted

1 teaspoon onion powder

1 teaspoon cayenne pepper

Salt and ground black pepper, to taste

2 garlic cloves, minced

1 cup cornmeal

1 cup green olives

Directions

In a plastic closeable bag, thoroughly combine all ingredients; shake to combine well.

Transfer the coated lobster tails to the greased cooking basket.

Cook in the preheated Air Fryer at 390 degrees for 6 to 7 minutes, shaking the basket halfway through. Work in batches.

Serve with green olives and enjoy!

Spicy Curried King Prawns

(Ready in about 10 minutes | Servings 2)

Per serving: 220 Calories; 9.7g Fat; 15.1g Carbs; 17.6g Protein; 2.2g Sugars

Ingredients

12 king prawns, rinsed

1 tablespoon coconut oil

1/2 teaspoon piri piri powder

Salt and ground black pepper, to taste

1 teaspoon garlic paste

1 teaspoon onion powder

1/2 teaspoon cumin powder

1 teaspoon curry powder

Directions

In a mixing bowl, toss all ingredient until the prawns are well coated on all sides.

Cook in the preheated Air Fryer at 360 degrees F for 4 minutes. Shake the basket and cook for 4 minutes more.

Serve over hot rice if desired. Bon appétit!

Korean-Style Salmon Patties

(Ready in about 15 minutes | Servings 4)

Per serving: 396 Calories; 20.1g Fat; 16.7g Carbs; 35.2g Protein; 3.1g Sugars

Ingredients

1 pound salmon

1 egg

1 garlic clove, minced

2 green onions, minced

1/2 cup rolled oats

Sauce:

1 teaspoon rice wine

1 ½ tablespoons soy sauce

1 teaspoon honey

A pinch of salt

1 teaspoon gochugaru (Korean red chili pepper flakes)

Directions

Start by preheating your Air Fryer to 380 degrees F. Spritz the Air Fryer basket with cooking oil.

Mix the salmon, egg, garlic, green onions, and rolled oats in a bowl; knead with your hands until everything is well incorporated.

Shape the mixture into equally sized patties. Transfer your patties to the Air Fryer basket.

Cook the fish patties for 10 minutes, turning them over halfway through.

Meanwhile, make the sauce by whisking all ingredients. Serve the warm fish patties with the sauce on the side.

English-Style Flounder Fillets

(Ready in about 20 minutes | Servings 2)
Per serving: 432 Calories; 16.7g Fat; 29g Carbs; 38.4g Protein; 2.7g Sugars

Ingredients

2 flounder fillets

1/4 cup all-purpose flour

1 egg

1/2 teaspoon Worcestershire sauce

1/2 cup bread crumbs

1/2 teaspoon lemon pepper

1/2 teaspoon coarse sea salt

1/4 teaspoon chili powder

Directions

Rinse and pat dry the flounder fillets.

Place the flour in a large pan.

Whisk the egg and Worcestershire sauce in a shallow bowl. In a separate bowl, mix the bread crumbs with the lemon pepper, salt, and chili powder.

Dredge the fillets in the flour, shaking off the excess. Then, dip them into the egg mixture. Lastly, coat the fish fillets with the breadcrumb mixture until they are coated on all sides.

Spritz with cooking spray and transfer to the Air Fryer basket. Cook at 390 degrees for 7 minutes. Turn them over, spritz with cooking spray on the other side, and cook another 5 minutes. Bon appétit!

Cod and Shallot Frittata

(Ready in about 20 minutes | Servings 3)
Per serving: 454 Calories; 30.8g Fat; 10.3g Carbs; 32.4g Protein; 4.1g Sugars

Ingredients

2 cod fillets

6 eggs

1/2 cup milk

1 shallot, chopped

2 garlic cloves, minced

Sea salt and ground black pepper, to taste

1/2 teaspoon red pepper flakes, crushed

Directions

Bring a pot of salted water to a boil. Boil the cod fillets for 5 minutes or until it is opaque. Flake the fish into bite-sized pieces.

In a mixing bowl, whisk the eggs and milk. Stir in the shallots, garlic, salt, black pepper, and red pepper flakes. Stir in the reserved fish.

Pour the mixture into the lightly greased baking pan.

Cook in the preheated Air Fryer at 360 degrees F for 9 minutes, flipping over halfway through. Bon appétit!

Crispy Tilapia Fillets

(Ready in about 20 minutes | Servings 5)

Per serving: 315 Calories; 9.1g Fat; 19.4g Carbs; 38.5g Protein; 0.7g Sugars

Ingredients

5 tablespoons all-purpose flour

Sea salt and white pepper, to taste

1 teaspoon garlic paste

2 tablespoons extra virgin olive oil

1/2 cup cornmeal

5 tilapia fillets, slice into halves

Directions

Combine the flour, salt, white pepper, garlic paste, olive oil, and cornmeal in a Ziploc bag. Add the fish fillets and shake to coat well.

Spritz the Air Fryer basket with cooking spray. Cook in the preheated Air Fryer at 400 degrees F for 10 minutes; turn them over and cook for 6 minutes more. Work in batches.

Serve with lemon wedges if desired. Enjoy!

Saucy Garam Masala Fish

(Ready in about 25 minutes | Servings 2)

Per serving: 301 Calories; 12.1g Fat; 2.3g Carbs; 43g Protein; 1.6g Sugars

Ingredients

2 teaspoons olive oil

1/4 cup coconut milk

1/2 teaspoon cayenne pepper

1 teaspoon Garam masala

1/4 teaspoon Kala namak (Indian black salt)

1/2 teaspoon fresh ginger, grated

1 garlic clove, minced

2 catfish fillets

1/4 cup coriander, roughly chopped

Directions

Preheat your Air Fryer to 390 degrees F. Then, spritz the baking dish with a nonstick cooking spray.

In a mixing bowl, whisk the olive oil, milk, cayenne pepper, Garam masala, Kala namak, ginger, and garlic.

Coat the catfish fillets with the Garam masala mixture. Cook the catfish fillets in the preheated Air Fryer approximately 18 minutes, turning over halfway through the cooking time.

Garnish with fresh coriander and serve over hot noodles if desired.

Grilled Salmon Steaks

(Ready in about 45 minutes | Servings 4)

Per serving: 420 Calories; 23g Fat; 2.5g Carbs; 48.5g Protein; 0.7g Sugars

Ingredients

2 cloves garlic, minced

4 tablespoons butter, melted

Sea salt and ground black pepper, to taste

1 teaspoon smoked paprika

1/2 teaspoon onion powder

1 tablespoon lime juice

1/4 cup dry white wine

4 salmon steaks

Directions

Place all ingredients in a large ceramic dish. Cover and let it marinate for 30 minutes in the refrigerator.

Arrange the salmon steaks on the grill pan. Bake at 390 degrees for 5 minutes, or until the salmon steaks are easily flaked with a fork.

Flip the fish steaks, baste with the reserved marinade, and cook another 5 minutes. Bon appétit!

Cajun Fish Cakes with Cheese

(Ready in about 30 minutes | Servings 4)

Per serving: 478 Calories; 30.1g Fat; 27.2g Carbs; 23.8g Protein; 2g Sugars

Ingredients

2 catfish fillets

1 cup all-purpose flour

3 ounces butter

1 teaspoon baking powder

1 teaspoon baking soda

1/2 cup buttermilk

1 teaspoon Cajun seasoning

1 cup Swiss cheese, shredded

Directions

Bring a pot of salted water to a boil. Boil the fish fillets for 5 minutes or until it is opaque. Flake the fish into small pieces.

Mix the remaining ingredients in a bowl; add the fish and mix until well combined. Shape the fish mixture into 12 patties.

Cook in the preheated Air Fryer at 380 degrees F for 15 minutes. Work in batches. Enjoy!

Smoked Halibut and Eggs in Brioche

(Ready in about 25 minutes | Servings 4)

Per serving: 372 Calories; 13.1g Fat; 22g Carbs; 38.6g Protein; 3.3g Sugars

Ingredients

4 brioche rolls

1 pound smoked halibut, chopped

4 eggs

1 teaspoon dried thyme

1 teaspoon dried basil

Salt and black pepper, to taste

Directions

Cut off the top of each brioche; then, scoop out the insides to make the shells.

Lay the prepared brioche shells in the lightly greased cooking basket.

Spritz with cooking oil; add the halibut. Crack an egg into each brioche shell; sprinkle with thyme, basil, salt, and black pepper.

Bake in the preheated Air Fryer at 325 degrees F for 20 minutes. Bon appétit!

Crab Cake Burgers

(Ready in about 2 hours 20 minutes | Servings 3)

Per serving: 500 Calories; 15.1g Fat; 51g Carbs; 44.3g Protein; 1.7g Sugars

Ingredients

2 eggs, beaten

1 shallot, chopped

2 garlic cloves, crushed

1 tablespoon olive oil

1 teaspoon yellow mustard

1 teaspoon fresh cilantro, chopped

10 ounces crab meat

1 cup tortilla chips, crushed

1/2 teaspoon cayenne pepper

1/2 teaspoon ground black pepper

Sea salt, to taste

3/4 cup fresh bread crumbs

Directions

In a mixing bowl, thoroughly combine the eggs, shallot, garlic, olive oil, mustard, cilantro, crab meat, tortilla chips, cayenne pepper, black pepper, and salt. Mix until well combined.

Shape the mixture into 6 patties. Dip the crab patties into the fresh breadcrumbs, coating well on all sides. Place in your refrigerator for 2 hours. Spritz the crab patties with cooking oil on both sides. Cook in the preheated Air Fryer at 360 degrees F for 14 minutes. Serve on dinner rolls if desired. Bon appétit!

Coconut Shrimp with Orange Sauce

(Ready in about 1 hour 30 minutes | Servings 3)
Per serving: 487 Calories; 21.7g Fat; 35.9g Carbs; 37.6g Protein; 8.4g Sugars

Ingredients

1 pound shrimp, cleaned and deveined
Sea salt and white pepper, to taste
1/2 cup all-purpose flour
1 egg
1/4 cup shredded coconut, unsweetened
3/2 cup fresh bread crumbs
2 tablespoons olive oil
1 lemon, cut into wedges
Dipping Sauce:
2 tablespoons butter
1/2 cup orange juice
2 tablespoons soy sauce
A pinch of salt
1/2 teaspoon tapioca starch
2 tablespoons fresh parsley, minced

Directions

Pat dry the shrimp and season them with salt and white pepper.

Place the flour on a large tray; then, whisk the egg in a shallow bowl. In a third shallow bowl, place the shredded coconut and breadcrumbs.

Dip the shrimp in the flour, then, dip in the egg. Lastly, coat the shrimp with the shredded coconut and bread crumbs. Refrigerate for 1 hour. Then, transfer to the cooking basket. Drizzle with olive oil and cook in the preheated Air Fryer at 370 degrees F for 6 minutes. Work in batches. Meanwhile, melt the butter in a small saucepan over medium-high heat; add the orange juice and bring it to a boil; reduce the heat and allow it to simmer approximately 7 minutes.

Add the soy sauce, salt, and tapioca; continue simmering until the sauce has thickened and reduced. Spoon the sauce over the shrimp and garnish with lemon wedges and parsley. Serve immediately.

Monkfish with Sautéed Vegetables and Olives

(Ready in about 20 minutes | Servings 2)
Per serving: 310 Calories; 13.3g Fat; 12.7g Carbs; 35.2g Protein; 5.4g Sugars

Ingredients

2 teaspoons olive oil
2 carrots, sliced
2 bell peppers, sliced
1 teaspoon dried thyme
1/2 teaspoon dried marjoram
1/2 teaspoon dried rosemary
2 monkfish fillets
1 tablespoon soy sauce
2 tablespoons lime juice
Coarse salt and ground black pepper, to taste
1 teaspoon cayenne pepper
1/2 cup Kalamata olives, pitted and sliced

Directions

In a nonstick skillet, heat the olive oil for 1 minute. Once hot, sauté the carrots and peppers until tender, about 4 minutes. Sprinkle with thyme, marjoram, and rosemary and set aside.

Toss the fish fillets with the soy sauce, lime juice, salt, black pepper, and cayenne pepper. Place the fish fillets in a lightly greased cooking basket and bake at 390 degrees F for 8 minutes.

Turn them over, add the olives, and cook an additional 4 minutes. Serve with the sautéed vegetables on the side. Bon appétit!

Delicious Snapper en Papillote

(Ready in about 20 minutes | Servings 2)

Per serving: 329 Calories; 9.8g Fat; 12.7g Carbs; 46.7g Protein; 5.4g Sugars

Ingredients

2 snapper fillets
1 shallot, peeled and sliced
2 garlic cloves, halved
1 bell pepper, sliced
1 small-sized serrano pepper, sliced
1 tomato, sliced
1 tablespoon olive oil
1/4 teaspoon freshly ground black pepper
1/2 teaspoon paprika
Sea salt, to taste
2 bay leaves

Directions

Place two parchment sheets on a working surface. Place the fish in the center of one side of the parchment paper.

Top with the shallot, garlic, peppers, and tomato. Drizzle olive oil over the fish and vegetables. Season with black pepper, paprika, and salt. Add the bay leaves.

Fold over the other half of the parchment. Now, fold the paper around the edges tightly and create a half moon shape, sealing the fish inside.

Cook in the preheated Air Fryer at 390 degrees F for 15 minutes. Serve warm.

Halibut Cakes with Horseradish Mayo

(Ready in about 20 minutes | Servings 4)

Per serving: 470 Calories; 38.2g Fat; 6.3g Carbs; 24.4g Protein; 1.5g Sugars

Ingredients

Halibut Cakes:

1 pound halibut
2 tablespoons olive oil
1/2 teaspoon cayenne pepper
1/4 teaspoon black pepper
Salt, to taste
2 tablespoons cilantro, chopped
1 shallot, chopped
2 garlic cloves, minced
1/2 cup Romano cheese, grated
1/2 cup breadcrumbs
1 egg, whisked
1 tablespoon Worcestershire sauce
Mayo Sauce:
1 teaspoon horseradish, grated
1/2 cup mayonnaise

Directions

Start by preheating your Air Fryer to 380 degrees F. Spritz the Air Fryer basket with cooking oil.

Mix all ingredients for the halibut cakes in a bowl; knead with your hands until everything is well incorporated.

Shape the mixture into equally sized patties. Transfer your patties to the Air Fryer basket. Cook the fish patties for 10 minutes, turning them over halfway through.

Mix the horseradish and mayonnaise. Serve the halibut cakes with the horseradish mayo. Bon appétit!

Dilled and Glazed Salmon Steaks

(Ready in about 20 minutes | Servings 2)

Per serving: 421 Calories; 16.8g Fat; 19.9g Carbs; 46.7g Protein; 18.1g Sugars

Ingredients

2 salmon steaks

Coarse sea salt, to taste

1/4 teaspoon freshly ground black pepper, or more to taste

2 tablespoons honey

1 tablespoon sesame oil

Zest of 1 lemon

1 tablespoon fresh lemon juice

1 teaspoon garlic, minced

1/2 teaspoon smoked cayenne pepper

1/2 teaspoon dried dill

Directions

Preheat your Air Fryer to 380 degrees F. Pat dry the salmon steaks with a kitchen towel.

In a ceramic dish, combine the remaining ingredients until everything is well whisked.

Add the salmon steaks to the ceramic dish and let them sit in the refrigerator for 1 hour. Now, place the salmon steaks in the cooking basket. Reserve the marinade.

Cook for 12 minutes, flipping halfway through the cooking time.

Meanwhile, cook the marinade in a small sauté pan over a moderate flame. Cook until the sauce has thickened.

Pour the sauce over the steaks and serve with mashed potatoes if desired. Bon appétit!

Easy Prawns alla Parmigiana

(Ready in about 20 minutes | Servings 4)

Per serving: 442 Calories; 10.3g Fat; 40.4g Carbs; 43.7g Protein; 1.2g Sugars

Ingredients

2 egg whites

1 cup all-purpose flour

1 cup Parmigiano-Reggiano, grated

1/2 cup fine breadcrumbs

1/2 teaspoon celery seeds

1/2 teaspoon porcini powder

1/2 teaspoon onion powder

1 teaspoon garlic powder

1/2 teaspoon dried rosemary

1/2 teaspoon sea salt

1/2 teaspoon ground black pepper

1 ½ pounds prawns, deveined

Directions

To make a breading station, whisk the egg whites in a shallow dish. In a separate dish, place the all-purpose flour.

In a third dish, thoroughly combine the Parmigiano-Reggiano, breadcrumbs, and seasonings; mix to combine well.

Dip the prawns in the flour, then, into the egg whites; lastly, dip them in the parm/breadcrumb mixture. Roll until they are covered on all sides.

Cook in the preheated Air Fryer at 390 degrees F for 5 to 7 minutes or until golden brown. Work in batches. Serve with lemon wedges if desired.

Indian Famous Fish Curry

(Ready in about 25 minutes | Servings 4)

Per serving: 449 Calories; 29.1g Fat; 20.4g Carbs; 27.3g Protein; 13.3g Sugars

Ingredients

2 tablespoons sunflower oil

1/2 pound fish, chopped

2 red chilies, chopped

1 tablespoon coriander powder

1 teaspoon curry paste

1 cup coconut milk

Salt and white pepper, to taste

1/2 teaspoon fenugreek seeds

1 shallot, minced

1 garlic clove, minced

1 ripe tomato, pureed

Directions

Preheat your Air Fryer to 380 degrees F; brush the cooking basket with 1 tablespoon of sunflower oil.

Cook your fish for 10 minutes on both sides. Transfer to the baking pan that is previously greased with the remaining tablespoon of sunflower oil.

Add the remaining ingredients and reduce the heat to 350 degrees F. Continue to cook an additional 10 to 12 minutes or until everything is heated through. Enjoy!

Cajun Cod Fillets with Avocado Sauce

(Ready in about 20 minutes | Servings 2)

Per serving: 418 Calories; 22.7g Fat; 12.5g Carbs; 40.1g Protein; 0.9g Sugars

Ingredients

2 cod fish fillets

1 egg

Sea salt, to taste

1/2 cup tortilla chips, crushed

2 teaspoons olive oil

1/2 avocado, peeled, pitted, and mashed

1 tablespoon mayonnaise

3 tablespoons sour cream

1/2 teaspoon yellow mustard

1 teaspoon lemon juice

1 garlic clove, minced

1/4 teaspoon black pepper

1/4 teaspoon salt

1/4 teaspoon hot pepper sauce

Directions

Start by preheating your Air Fryer to 360 degrees F. Spritz the Air Fryer basket with cooking oil.

Pat dry the fish fillets with a kitchen towel. Beat the egg in a shallow bowl.

In a separate bowl, thoroughly combine the salt, crushed tortilla chips, and olive oil.

Dip the fish into the egg, then, into the crumb mixture, making sure to coat thoroughly. Cook in the preheated Air Fryer approximately 12 minutes.

Meanwhile, make the avocado sauce by mixing the remaining ingredients in a bowl. Place in your refrigerator until ready to serve.

Serve the fish fillets with chilled avocado sauce on the side. Bon appétit!

Old Bay Calamari

(Ready in about 20 minutes + marinating time | Servings 3)

Per serving: 448 Calories; 5.3g Fat; 58.9g Carbs; 31.9g Protein; 0.2g Sugars

Ingredients

1 cup beer

1 pound squid, cleaned and cut into rings

1 cup all-purpose flour

2 eggs

1/2 cup cornstarch

Sea salt, to taste

1/2 teaspoon ground black pepper

1 tablespoon Old Bay seasoning

Directions

Add the beer and squid in a glass bowl, cover and let it sit in your refrigerator for 1 hour.

Preheat your Air Fryer to 390 degrees F. Rinse the squid and pat it dry.

Place the flour in a shallow bowl. In another bowl, whisk the eggs. Add the cornstarch and seasonings to a third shallow bowl.

Dredge the calamari in the flour. Then, dip them into the egg mixture; finally, coat them with the cornstarch on all sided.

Arrange them in the cooking basket. Spritz with cooking oil and cook for 9 to 12 minutes, depending on the desired level of doneness. Work in batches.

Serve warm with your favorite dipping sauce. Enjoy!

Crispy Mustardy Fish Fingers

(Ready in about 20 minutes | Servings 4)
Per serving: 468 Calories; 12.7g Fat; 45.6g Carbs; 41.9g Protein; 1.4g Sugars

Ingredients

1 ½ pounds tilapia pieces (fingers)
1/2 cup all-purpose flour
2 eggs
1 tablespoon yellow mustard
1 cup cornmeal
1 teaspoon garlic powder
1 teaspoon onion powder
Sea salt and ground black pepper, to taste
1/2 teaspoon celery powder
2 tablespoons peanut oil

Directions

Pat dry the fish fingers with a kitchen towel.

To make a breading station, place the all-purpose flour in a shallow dish. In a separate dish, whisk the eggs with mustard.

In a third bowl, mix the remaining ingredients. Dredge the fish fingers in the flour, shaking the excess into the bowl; dip in the egg mixture and

turn to coat evenly; then, dredge in the cornmeal mixture, turning a couple of times to coat evenly. Cook in the preheated Air Fryer at 390 degrees F for 5 minutes; turn them over and cook another 5 minutes. Enjoy!

Greek-Style Roast Fish

(Ready in about 20 minutes | Servings 3)
Per serving: 345 Calories; 32.7g Fat; 8.4g Carbs; 45.9g Protein; 3.5g Sugars

Ingredients

2 tablespoons olive oil
1 red onion, sliced
2 cloves garlic, chopped
1 Florina pepper, deveined and minced
3 pollock fillets, skinless
2 ripe tomatoes, diced
12 Kalamata olives, pitted and chopped
2 tablespoons capers
1 teaspoon oregano
1 teaspoon rosemary
Sea salt, to taste
1/2 cup white wine

Directions

Start by preheating your Air Fryer to 360 degrees F. Heat the oil in a baking pan. Once hot, sauté the onion, garlic, and pepper for 2 to 3 minutes or until fragrant.

Add the fish fillets to the baking pan. Top with the tomatoes, olives, and capers. Sprinkle with the oregano, rosemary, and salt. Pour in white wine and transfer to the cooking basket.

Turn the temperature to 395 degrees F and bake for 10 minutes. Taste for seasoning and serve on individual plates, garnished with some extra Mediterranean herbs if desired. Enjoy!

Quick-Fix Seafood Breakfast

(Ready in about 30 minutes | Servings 2)

Per serving: 414 Calories; 23.4g Fat; 11.6g Carbs; 38.8g Protein; 7.2g Sugars

Ingredients

1 tablespoon olive oil

2 garlic cloves, minced

1 small yellow onion, chopped

1/4 pound tilapia pieces

1/4 pound rockfish pieces

1/2 teaspoon dried basil

Salt and white pepper, to taste

4 eggs, lightly beaten

1 tablespoon dry sherry

4 tablespoons cheese, shredded

Directions

Start by preheating your Air Fryer to 350 degrees F; add the olive oil to a baking pan. Once hot, cook the garlic and onion for 2 minutes or until fragrant.

Add the fish, basil, salt, and pepper. In a mixing dish, thoroughly combine the eggs with sherry and cheese. Pour the mixture into the baking pan. Cook at 360 degrees F approximately 20 minutes. Bon appétit!

Snapper Casserole with Gruyere Cheese

(Ready in about 25 minutes | Servings 4)

Per serving: 406 Calories; 19.9g Fat; 9.3g Carbs; 46.4g Protein; 4.5g Sugars

Ingredients

2 tablespoons olive oil

1 shallot, thinly sliced

2 garlic cloves, minced

1 ½ pounds snapper fillets

Sea salt and ground black pepper, to taste

1 teaspoon cayenne pepper

1/2 teaspoon dried basil

1/2 cup tomato puree

1/2 cup white wine

1 cup Gruyere cheese, shredded

Directions

Heat 1 tablespoon of olive oil in a saucepan over medium-high heat. Now, cook the shallot and garlic until tender and aromatic.

Preheat your Air Fryer to 370 degrees F.

Grease a casserole dish with 1 tablespoon of olive oil. Place the snapper fillet in the casserole dish. Season with salt, black pepper, and cayenne pepper. Add the sautéed shallot mixture.

Add the basil, tomato puree and wine to the casserole dish. Cook for 10 minutes in the preheated Air Fryer.

Top with the shredded cheese and cook an additional 7 minutes. Serve immediately.

VEGETABLES & SIDE DISHES

Easy Veggie Fried Balls

(Ready in about 30 minutes | Servings 3)

Per serving: 364 Calories; 13.7g Fat; 48.3g Carbs; 14g Protein; 5.3g Sugars

Ingredients

1/2 pound sweet potatoes, grated

1 cup carrots

1 cup corn

2 garlic cloves, minced

1 shallot, chopped

Sea salt and ground black pepper, to taste

2 tablespoons fresh parsley, chopped

1 egg, well beaten

1/2 cup purpose flour

1/2 cup Romano cheese, grated

1/2 cup dried bread flakes

1 tablespoon olive oil

Directions

Mix the veggies, spices, egg, flour, and Romano cheese until everything is well incorporated.

Take 1 tablespoon of the veggie mixture and roll into a ball. Roll the balls onto the dried bread flakes. Brush the veggie balls with olive oil on all sides.

Cook in the preheated Air Fryer at 360 degrees F for 15 minutes or until thoroughly cooked and crispy.

Repeat the process until you run out of ingredients. Bon appétit!

Fried Peppers with Sriracha Mayo

(Ready in about 20 minutes | Servings 2)

Per serving: 346 Calories; 34.1g Fat; 9.5g Carbs; 2.3g Protein; 4.9g Sugars

Ingredients

4 bell peppers, seeded and sliced (1-inch pieces)

1 onion, sliced (1-inch pieces)

1 tablespoon olive oil

1/2 teaspoon dried rosemary

1/2 teaspoon dried basil

Kosher salt, to taste

1/4 teaspoon ground black pepper

1/3 cup mayonnaise

1/3 teaspoon Sriracha

Directions

Toss the bell peppers and onions with the olive oil, rosemary, basil, salt, and black pepper.

Place the peppers and onions on an even layer in the cooking basket. Cook at 400 degrees F for 12 to 14 minutes.

Meanwhile, make the sauce by whisking the mayonnaise and Sriracha. Serve immediately.

Classic Fried Pickles

(Ready in about 20 minutes | Servings 2)

Per serving: 342 Calories; 28.5g Fat; 12.5g Carbs; 9.1g Protein; 4.9g Sugars

Ingredients

1 egg, whisked

2 tablespoons buttermilk

1/2 cup fresh breadcrumbs

1/4 cup Romano cheese, grated

1/2 teaspoon onion powder

1/2 teaspoon garlic powder

1 ½ cups dill pickle chips, pressed dry with kitchen towels

Mayo Sauce:

1/4 cup mayonnaise

1/2 tablespoon mustard

1/2 teaspoon molasses

1 tablespoon ketchup

1/4 teaspoon ground black pepper

Directions

In a shallow bowl, whisk the egg with buttermilk. In another bowl, mix the breadcrumbs, cheese, onion powder, and garlic powder.

Dredge the pickle chips in the egg mixture, then, in the breadcrumb/cheese mixture.

Cook in the preheated Air Fryer at 400 degrees F for 5 minutes; shake the basket and cook for 5 minutes more.

Meanwhile, mix all the sauce ingredients until well combined. Serve the fried pickles with the mayo sauce for dipping.

Fried Green Beans with Pecorino Romano

(Ready in about 15 minutes | Servings 3)

Per serving: 340 Calories; 9.7g Fat; 50.9g Carbs; 12.8g Protein; 4.7g Sugars

Ingredients

2 tablespoons buttermilk

1 egg

4 tablespoons cornmeal

4 tablespoons tortilla chips, crushed

4 tablespoons Pecorino Romano cheese, finely grated

Coarse salt and crushed black pepper, to taste

1 teaspoon smoked paprika

12 ounces green beans, trimmed

Directions

In a shallow bowl, whisk together the buttermilk and egg.

In a separate bowl, combine the cornmeal, tortilla chips, Pecorino Romano cheese, salt, black pepper, and paprika.

Dip the green beans in the egg mixture, then, in the cornmeal/cheese mixture. Place the green beans in the lightly greased cooking basket.

Cook in the preheated Air Fryer at 390 degrees F for 4 minutes. Shake the basket and cook for a further 3 minutes.

Taste, adjust the seasonings, and serve with the dipping sauce if desired. Bon appétit!

Spicy Roasted Potatoes

(Ready in about 15 minutes | Servings 2)

Per serving: 299 Calories; 13.6g Fat; 40.9g Carbs; 4.8g Protein; 1.4g Sugars

Ingredients

4 potatoes, peeled and cut into wedges

2 tablespoons olive oil

Sea salt and ground black pepper, to taste

1 teaspoon cayenne pepper

1/2 teaspoon ancho chili powder

Directions

Toss all ingredients in a mixing bowl until the potatoes are well covered.

Transfer them to the Air Fryer basket and cook at 400 degrees F for 6 minutes; shake the basket and cook for a further 6 minutes.

Serve warm with your favorite sauce for dipping. Bon appétit!

Spicy Glazed Carrots

(Ready in about 20 minutes | Servings 3)

Per serving: 162 Calories; 9.3g Fat; 20.1g Carbs; 1.4g Protein; 12.8g Sugars

Ingredients

1 pound carrots, cut into matchsticks

2 tablespoons peanut oil

1 tablespoon agave syrup

1 jalapeño, seeded and minced

1/4 teaspoon dill

1/2 teaspoon basil

Salt and white pepper to taste

Directions

Start by preheating your Air Fryer to 380 degrees F.

Toss all ingredients together and place them in the Air Fryer basket.

Cook for 15 minutes, shaking the basket halfway through the cooking time. Transfer to a serving platter and enjoy!

Easy Sweet Potato Bake

(Ready in about 35 minutes | Servings 3)

Per serving: 409 Calories; 26.1g Fat; 38.3g Carbs; 7.2g Protein; 10.9g Sugars

Ingredients

1 stick butter, melted

1 pound sweet potatoes, mashed

2 tablespoons honey

2 eggs, beaten

1/3 cup coconut milk

1/4 cup flour

1/2 cup fresh breadcrumbs

Directions

Start by preheating your Air Fryer to 325 degrees F.

Spritz a casserole dish with cooking oil.

In a mixing bowl, combine all ingredients, except for the breadcrumbs and 1 tablespoon of butter. Spoon the mixture into the prepared casserole dish.

Top with the breadcrumbs and brush the top with the remaining 1 tablespoon of butter. Bake in the preheated Air Fryer for 30 minutes. Bon appétit!

Avocado Fries with Roasted Garlic Mayonnaise

(Ready in about 50 minutes | Servings 4)

Per serving: 351 Calories; 27.7g Fat; 21.5g Carbs; 6.4g Protein; 1.1g Sugars

Ingredients

1/2 head garlic (6-7 cloves)

3/4 cup all-purpose flour

Sea salt and ground black pepper, to taste

2 eggs

1 cup tortilla chips, crushed

3 avocados, cut into wedges

Sauce:

1/2 cup mayonnaise

1 teaspoon lemon juice

1 teaspoon mustard

Directions

Place the garlic on a piece of aluminum foil and spritz with cooking spray. Wrap the garlic in the foil.

Cook in the preheated Air Fryer at 400 degrees for 12 minutes. Check the garlic, open the top of the foil and continue to cook for 10 minutes more. Let it cool for 10 to 15 minutes; remove the cloves by squeezing them out of the skins; mash the garlic and reserve.

In a shallow bowl, combine the flour, salt, and black pepper. In another shallow dish, whisk the eggs until frothy.

Place the crushed tortilla chips in a third shallow dish. Dredge the avocado wedges in the flour mixture, shaking off the excess. Then, dip in the egg mixture; lastly, dredge in crushed tortilla chips.

Spritz the avocado wedges with cooking oil on all sides.

Cook in the preheated Air Fryer at 395 degrees F approximately 8 minutes, turning them over halfway through the cooking time.

Meanwhile, combine the sauce ingredients with the smashed roasted garlic. To serve, divide the avocado fries between plates and top with the sauce. Enjoy!

Roasted Broccoli with Sesame Seeds

(Ready in about 15 minutes | Servings 2)
Per serving: 267 Calories; 19.5g Fat; 20.2g Carbs; 8.9g Protein; 5.2g Sugars

Ingredients

1 pound broccoli florets
2 tablespoons sesame oil
1/2 teaspoon shallot powder
1/2 teaspoon porcini powder
1 teaspoon garlic powder
Sea salt and ground black pepper, to taste
1/2 teaspoon cumin powder
1/4 teaspoon paprika
2 tablespoons sesame seeds

Directions

Start by preheating the Air Fryer to 400 degrees F.

Blanch the broccoli in salted boiling water until al dente, about 3 to 4 minutes. Drain well and transfer to the lightly greased Air Fryer basket.

Add the sesame oil, shallot powder, porcini powder, garlic powder, salt, black pepper, cumin powder, paprika, and sesame seeds.

Cook for 6 minutes, tossing halfway through the cooking time. Bon appétit!

Corn on the Cob with Herb Butter

(Ready in about 15 minutes | Servings 2)
Per serving: 239 Calories; 13.3g Fat; 30.2g Carbs; 5.4g Protein; 5.8g Sugars

Ingredients

2 ears fresh corn, shucked and cut into halves
2 tablespoons butter, room temperature
1 teaspoon granulated garlic
1/2 teaspoon fresh ginger, grated
Sea salt and ground black pepper, to taste
1 tablespoon fresh rosemary, chopped
1 tablespoon fresh basil, chopped
2 tablespoons fresh chives, roughly chopped

Directions

Spritz the corn with cooking spray. Cook at 395 degrees F for 6 minutes, turning them over halfway through the cooking time.

In the meantime, mix the butter with the granulated garlic, ginger, salt, black pepper, rosemary, and basil.

Spread the butter mixture all over the corn on the cob. Cook in the preheated Air Fryer an additional 2 minutes. Bon appétit!

Rainbow Vegetable Fritters

(Ready in about 20 minutes | Servings 2)

Per serving: 215 Calories; 8.4g Fat; 31.6g Carbs; 6g Protein; 4.1g Sugars

Ingredients

1 zucchini, grated and squeezed

1 cup corn kernels

1/2 cup canned green peas

4 tablespoons all-purpose flour

2 tablespoons fresh shallots, minced

1 teaspoon fresh garlic, minced

1 tablespoon peanut oil

Sea salt and ground black pepper, to taste

1 teaspoon cayenne pepper

Directions

In a mixing bowl, thoroughly combine all ingredients until everything is well incorporated. Shape the mixture into patties. Spritz the Air Fryer basket with cooking spray.

Cook in the preheated Air Fryer at 365 degrees F for 6 minutes. Turn them over and cook for a further 6 minutes

Serve immediately and enjoy!

Mediterranean Vegetable Skewers

(Ready in about 30 minutes | Servings 4)

Per serving: 138 Calories; 10.2g Fat; 10.2g Carbs; 2.2g Protein; 6.6g Sugars

Ingredients

2 medium-sized zucchini, cut into 1-inch pieces

2 red bell peppers, cut into 1-inch pieces

1 green bell pepper, cut into 1-inch pieces

1 red onion, cut into 1-inch pieces

2 tablespoons olive oil

Sea salt, to taste

1/2 teaspoon black pepper, preferably freshly cracked

1/2 teaspoon red pepper flakes

Directions

Soak the wooden skewers in water for 15 minutes. Thread the vegetables on skewers; drizzle olive oil all over the vegetable skewers; sprinkle with spices.

Cook in the preheated Air Fryer at 400 degrees F for 13 minutes. Serve warm and enjoy!

Roasted Veggies with Yogurt-Tahini Sauce

(Ready in about 20 minutes | Servings 4)

Per serving: 254 Calories; 17.2g Fat; 19.6g Carbs; 11.1g Protein; 8.1g Sugars

Ingredients

1 pound Brussels sprouts

1 pound button mushrooms

2 tablespoons olive oil

1/2 teaspoon white pepper

1/2 teaspoon dried dill weed

1/2 teaspoon cayenne pepper

1/2 teaspoon celery seeds

1/2 teaspoon mustard seeds

Salt, to taste

Yogurt Tahini Sauce:

1 cup plain yogurt

2 heaping tablespoons tahini paste

1 tablespoon lemon juice

1 tablespoon extra-virgin olive oil

1/2 teaspoon Aleppo pepper, minced

Directions

Toss the Brussels sprouts and mushrooms with olive oil and spices. Preheat your Air Fryer to 380 degrees F.

Add the Brussels sprouts to the cooking basket and cook for 10 minutes.

Add the mushrooms, turn the temperature to 390 degrees and cook for 6 minutes more.

While the vegetables are cooking, make the sauce by whisking all ingredients. Serve the warm vegetables with the sauce on the side. Bon appétit!

Swiss Cheese & Vegetable Casserole

(Ready in about 50 minutes | Servings 4)
Per serving: 328 Calories; 16.5g Fat; 33.1g Carbs; 13.1g Protein; 7.6g Sugars

Ingredients

1 pound potatoes, peeled and sliced (1/4-inch thick)
2 tablespoons olive oil
1/2 teaspoon red pepper flakes, crushed
1/2 teaspoon freshly ground black pepper
Salt, to taste
3 bell peppers, thinly sliced
1 serrano pepper, thinly sliced
2 medium-sized tomatoes, sliced
1 leek, thinly sliced
2 garlic cloves, minced
1 cup Swiss cheese, shredded

Directions

Start by preheating your Air Fryer to 350 degrees F. Spritz a casserole dish with cooking oil.

Place the potatoes in the casserole dish in an even layer; drizzle 1 tablespoon of olive oil over the top. Then, add the red pepper, black pepper, and salt. Add 2 bell peppers and 1/2 of the leeks. Add the tomatoes and the remaining 1 tablespoon of olive oil.

Add the remaining peppers, leeks, and minced garlic. Top with the cheese.

Cover the casserole with foil and bake for 32 minutes. Remove the foil and increase the temperature to 400 degrees F; bake an additional 16 minutes. Bon appétit!

Easy Sweet Potato Hash Browns

(Ready in about 50 minutes | Servings 2)
Per serving: 381 Calories; 16.7g Fat; 44.8g Carbs; 14.3g Protein; 3.9g Sugars

Ingredients

1 pound sweet potatoes, peeled and grated
2 eggs, whisked
1/4 cup scallions, chopped
1 teaspoon fresh garlic, minced
Sea salt and ground black pepper, to taste
1/4 teaspoon ground allspice
1/2 teaspoon cinnamon
1 tablespoon peanut oil

Directions

Allow the sweet potatoes to soak for 25 minutes in cold water. Drain the water; dry the sweet potatoes with a kitchen towel.

Add the remaining ingredients and stir to combine well.

Cook in the preheated Air Fryer at 395 degrees F for 20 minutes. Shake the basket once or twice. Serve with ketchup.

American-Style Brussel Sprout Salad

(Ready in about 35 minutes | Servings 4)
Per serving: 319 Calories; 18.5g Fat; 27g Carbs; 14.7g Protein; 14.6g Sugars

Ingredients

1 pound Brussels sprouts
1 apple, cored and diced
1/2 cup mozzarella cheese, crumbled

1/2 cup pomegranate seeds

1 small-sized red onion, chopped

4 eggs, hardboiled and sliced

Dressing:

1/4 cup olive oil

2 tablespoons champagne vinegar

1 teaspoon Dijon mustard

1 teaspoon honey

Sea salt and ground black pepper, to taste

Directions

Start by preheating your Air Fryer to 380 degrees F.

Add the Brussels sprouts to the cooking basket. Spritz with cooking spray and cook for 15 minutes. Let it cool to room temperature about 15 minutes.

Toss the Brussels sprouts with the apple, cheese, pomegranate seeds, and red onion.

Mix all ingredients for the dressing and toss to combine well. Serve topped with the hard-boiled eggs. Bon appétit!

The Best Cauliflower Tater Tots

(Ready in about 25 minutes | Servings 4)

Per serving: 267 Calories; 19.2g Fat; 9.6g Carbs; 14.9g Protein; 2.9g Sugars

Ingredients

1 pound cauliflower florets

2 eggs

1 tablespoon olive oil

2 tablespoons scallions, chopped

1 garlic clove, minced

1 cup Colby cheese, shredded

1/2 cup breadcrumbs

Sea salt and ground black pepper, to taste

1/4 teaspoon dried dill weed

1 teaspoon paprika

Directions

Blanch the cauliflower in salted boiling water about 3 to 4 minutes until al dente. Drain well and pulse in a food processor.

Add the remaining ingredients; mix to combine well. Shape the cauliflower mixture into bite-sized tots.

Spritz the Air Fryer basket with cooking spray. Cook in the preheated Air Fryer at 375 degrees F for 16 minutes, shaking halfway through the cooking time. Serve with your favorite sauce for dipping. Bon appétit!

Skinny Pumpkin Chips

(Ready in about 20 minutes | Servings 2)

Per serving: 118 Calories; 7g Fat; 14.7g Carbs; 2.2g Protein; 6.2g Sugars

Ingredients

1 pound pumpkin, cut into sticks

1 tablespoon coconut oil

1/2 teaspoon rosemary

1/2 teaspoon basil

Salt and ground black pepper, to taste

Directions

Start by preheating the Air Fryer to 395 degrees F. Brush the pumpkin sticks with coconut oil; add the spices and toss to combine.

Cook for 13 minutes, shaking the basket halfway through the cooking time.

Serve with mayonnaise. Bon appétit!

Cheese Stuffed Roasted Peppers

(Ready in about 20 minutes | Servings 2)

Per serving: 367 Calories; 21.8g Fat; 21.9g Carbs; 21.5g Protein; 14.1g Sugars

Ingredients

2 red bell peppers, tops and seeds removed

2 yellow bell peppers, tops and seeds removed

Salt and pepper, to taste

1 cup cream cheese

4 tablespoons mayonnaise

2 pickles, chopped

Directions

Arrange the peppers in the lightly greased cooking basket. Cook in the preheated Air Fryer at 400 degrees F for 15 minutes, turning them over halfway through the cooking time.

Season with salt and pepper.

Then, in a mixing bowl, combine the cream cheese with the mayonnaise and chopped pickles. Stuff the pepper with the cream cheese mixture and serve. Enjoy!

Three-Cheese Stuffed Mushrooms

(Ready in about 15 minutes | Servings 3)

Per serving: 345 Calories; 28g Fat; 11.2g Carbs; 14.4g Protein; 8.1g Sugars

Ingredients

9 large button mushrooms, stems removed

1 tablespoon olive oil

Salt and ground black pepper, to taste

1/2 teaspoon dried rosemary

6 tablespoons Swiss cheese shredded

6 tablespoons Romano cheese, shredded

6 tablespoons cream cheese

1 teaspoon soy sauce

1 teaspoon garlic, minced

3 tablespoons green onion, minced

Directions

Brush the mushroom caps with olive oil; sprinkle with salt, pepper, and rosemary.

In a mixing bowl, thoroughly combine the remaining ingredients; mix to combine well and divide the filling mixture among the mushroom caps.

Cook in the preheated Air Fryer at 390 degrees F for 7 minutes.

Let the mushrooms cool slightly before serving. Bon appétit!

Sweet Potato Chips with Greek Yogurt Dip

(Ready in about 20 minutes | Servings 2)

Per serving: 378 Calories; 13.9g Fat; 55.2g Carbs; 9.4g Protein; 12.6g Sugars

Ingredients

4 sweet potatoes, sliced

2 tablespoons olive oil

Coarse sea salt and freshly ground black pepper, to taste

1 teaspoon paprika

Dipping Sauce:

1/2 cup Greek-style yogurt

1 clove garlic, minced

1 tablespoon fresh chives, chopped

Directions

Soak the sweet potato slices in icy cold water for 20 to 30 minutes. Drain the sweet potatoes and pat them dry with kitchen towels.

Toss the sweet potato slices with olive oil, salt, black pepper, and paprika.

Place in the lightly greased cooking basket. Cook in the preheated Air Fryer at 360 degrees F for 14 minutes.

Meanwhile, make the sauce by whisking the remaining ingredients. Serve the sweet potato chips with the sauce for dipping and enjoy!

Classic Onion Rings

(Ready in about 30 minutes | Servings 2)

Per serving: 440 Calories; 12.7g Fat; 60g Carbs; 19.2g Protein; 5.6g Sugars

Ingredients

1 medium-sized onion, slice into rings

1 cup all-purpose flour

1 teaspoon baking powder

Coarse sea salt and ground black pepper, to your liking

1/2 cup yogurt

2 eggs, beaten

3/4 cup bread crumbs

1 teaspoon onion powder

1 teaspoon garlic powder

1/2 teaspoon celery seeds

Directions

Place the onion rings in the bowl with cold water; let them soak approximately 20 minutes; drain the onion rings and pat dry using a pepper towel. In a shallow bowl, mix the flour, baking powder, salt, and black pepper. Add the yogurt and eggs and mix well to combine.

In another shallow bowl, mix the bread crumbs, onion powder, garlic powder, and celery seeds. Dip the onion rings in the flour/egg mixture; then, dredge in the breadcrumb mixture.

Spritz the Air Fryer basket with cooking spray; arrange the breaded onion rings in the basket.

Cook in the preheated Air Fryer at 400 degrees F for 4 to 5 minutes, turning them over halfway through the cooking time. Bon appétit!

Greek-Style Roasted Tomatoes with Feta

(Ready in about 20 minutes | Servings 2)

Per serving: 148 Calories; 9.4g Fat; 9.4g Carbs; 7.8g Protein; 6.6g Sugars

Ingredients

3 medium-sized tomatoes, cut into four slices, pat dry

1 teaspoon dried basil

1 teaspoon dried oregano

1/4 teaspoon red pepper flakes, crushed

1/2 teaspoon sea salt

3 slices Feta cheese

Directions

Spritz the tomatoes with cooking oil and transfer them to the Air Fryer basket. Sprinkle with seasonings.

Cook at 350 degrees F approximately 8 minutes turning them over halfway through the cooking time.

Top with the cheese and cook an additional 4 minutes. Bon appétit!

Sweet Corn Fritters with Avocado

(Ready in about 20 minutes | Servings 3)

Per serving: 383 Calories; 21.3g Fat; 42.8g Carbs; 12.7g Protein; 9.2g Sugars

Ingredients

2 cups sweet corn kernels

1 small-sized onion, chopped

1 garlic clove, minced

2 eggs, whisked

1 teaspoon baking powder

2 tablespoons fresh cilantro, chopped

Sea salt and ground black pepper, to taste

1 avocado, peeled, pitted and diced

2 tablespoons sweet chili sauce

Directions

In a mixing bowl, thoroughly combine the corn, onion, garlic, eggs, baking powder, cilantro, salt, and black pepper.

Shape the corn mixture into 6 patties and transfer them to the lightly greased Air Fryer basket.

Cook in the preheated Air Fry at 370 degrees for 8 minutes; turn them over and cook for 7 minutes longer.

Serve the fritters with the avocado and chili sauce.

Cauliflower and Goat Cheese Croquettes

(Ready in about 30 minutes | Servings 2)
Per serving: 297 Calories; 21.7g Fat; 11.7g Carbs; 15.3g Protein; 2.6g Sugars

Ingredients

1/2 pound cauliflower florets
2 garlic cloves, minced
1 cup goat cheese, shredded
Sea salt and ground black pepper, to taste
1/2 teaspoon shallot powder
1/4 teaspoon cumin powder
1 cup sour cream
1 teaspoon Dijon mustard

Directions

Place the cauliflower florets in a saucepan of water; bring to the boil; reduce the heat and cook for 10 minutes or until tender.

Mash the cauliflower using your blender; add the garlic, cheese, and spices; mix to combine well.

Form the cauliflower mixture into croquettes shapes.

Cook in the preheated Air Fryer at 375 degrees F for 16 minutes, shaking halfway through the cooking time. Serve with the sour cream and mustard. Bon appétit!

Greek-Style Vegetable Bake

(Ready in about 35 minutes | Servings 4)
Per serving: 296 Calories; 22.9g Fat; 16.1g Carbs; 9.3g Protein; 9.9g Sugars

Ingredients

1 eggplant, peeled and sliced
2 bell peppers, seeded and sliced
1 red onion, sliced
1 teaspoon fresh garlic, minced
4 tablespoons olive oil
1 teaspoon mustard
1 teaspoon dried oregano
1 teaspoon smoked paprika
Salt and ground black pepper, to taste
1 tomato, sliced
6 ounces halloumi cheese, sliced lengthways

Directions

Start by preheating your Air Fryer to 370 degrees F. Spritz a baking pan with nonstick cooking spray.

Place the eggplant, peppers, onion, and garlic on the bottom of the baking pan. Add the olive oil, mustard, and spices. Transfer to the cooking basket and cook for 14 minutes.

Top with the tomatoes and cheese; increase the temperature to 390 degrees F and cook for 5 minutes more until bubbling. Let it sit on a cooling rack for 10 minutes before serving.

Bon appétit!

Japanese Tempura Bowl

(Ready in about 20 minutes | Servings 3)

Per serving: 446 Calories; 14.7g Fat; 63.5g Carbs; 14.6g Protein; 3.8g Sugars

Ingredients

1 cup all-purpose flour
Kosher salt and ground black pepper, to taste
1/2 teaspoon paprika
2 eggs
3 tablespoons soda water
1 cup panko crumbs
2 tablespoons olive oil
1 cup green beans
1 onion, cut into rings
1 zucchini, cut into slices
2 tablespoons soy sauce
1 tablespoon mirin
1 teaspoon dashi granules

Directions

In a shallow bowl, mix the flour, salt, black pepper, and paprika. In a separate bowl, whisk the eggs and soda water. In a third shallow bowl, combine the panko crumbs with olive oil.

Dip the vegetables in flour mixture, then in the egg mixture; lastly, roll over the panko mixture to coat evenly.

Cook in the preheated Air Fryer at 400 degrees F for 10 minutes, shaking the basket halfway through the cooking time. Work in batches until the vegetables are crispy and golden brown.

Then, make the sauce by whisking the soy sauce, mirin, and dashi granules. Bon appétit!

Balsamic Root Vegetables

(Ready in about 25 minutes | Servings 3)

Per serving: 405 Calories; 9.7g Fat; 74.7g Carbs; 7.7g Protein; 15.2g Sugars

Ingredients

2 potatoes, cut into 1 1/2-inch pieces
2 carrots, cut into 1 1/2-inch pieces
2 parsnips, cut into 1 1/2-inch pieces
1 onion, cut into 1 1/2-inch pieces
Pink Himalayan salt and ground black pepper, to taste
1/4 teaspoon smoked paprika
1 teaspoon garlic powder
1/2 teaspoon dried thyme
1/2 teaspoon dried marjoram
2 tablespoons olive oil
2 tablespoons balsamic vinegar

Directions

Toss all ingredients in a large mixing dish.

Roast in the preheated Air Fryer at 400 degrees F for 10 minutes. Shake the basket and cook for 7 minutes more.

Serve with some extra fresh herbs if desired. Bon appétit!

SNACKS & APPETIZERS

Baby Carrots with Asian Flair

(Ready in about 20 minutes | Servings 3)

Per serving: 165 Calories; 9.3g Fat; 20.6g Carbs; 1.6g Protein; 11.8g Sugars

Ingredients

1 pound baby carrots

2 tablespoons sesame oil

1/2 teaspoon Szechuan pepper

1 teaspoon Wuxiang powder (Five-spice powder)

1 tablespoon honey

1 large garlic clove, crushed

1 (1-inch) piece fresh ginger root, peeled and grated

2 tablespoons tamari sauce

Directions

Start by preheating your Air Fryer to 380 degrees F.

Toss all ingredients together and place them in the Air Fryer basket.

Cook for 15 minutes, shaking the basket halfway through the cooking time. Enjoy!

Mexican-Style Corn on the Cob with Bacon

(Ready in about 20 minutes | Servings 4)

Per serving: 261 Calories; 14.2g Fat; 32.5g Carbs; 7.4g Protein; 5.1g Sugars

Ingredients

2 slices bacon

4 ears fresh corn, shucked and cut into halves

1 avocado, pitted, peeled and mashed

1 teaspoon ancho chili powder

2 garlic cloves

2 tablespoons cilantro, chopped

1 teaspoon lime juice

Salt and black pepper, to taste

Directions

Start by preheating your Air Fryer to 400 degrees F. Cook the bacon for 6 to 7 minutes; chop into small chunks and reserve.

Spritz the corn with cooking spray. Cook at 395 degrees F for 8 minutes, turning them over halfway through the cooking time.

Mix the reserved bacon with the remaining ingredients. Spoon the bacon mixture over the corn on the cob and serve immediately. Bon appétit!

Beer Battered Vidalia Rings

(Ready in about 30 minutes | Servings 4)

Per serving: 318 Calories; 10.7g Fat; 43.9g Carbs; 9.4g Protein; 5.2g Sugars

Ingredients

1/2 pound Vidalia onions, sliced into rings

1/2 cup all-purpose flour

1/4 cup cornmeal

1/2 teaspoon baking powder

Sea salt and freshly cracked black pepper, to taste

1/4 teaspoon garlic powder

2 eggs, beaten

1/2 cup lager-style beer

1 cup plain breadcrumbs

2 tablespoons peanut oil

Directions

Place the onion rings in the bowl with icy cold water; let them soak approximately 20 minutes; drain the onion rings and pat them dry.

In a shallow bowl, mix the flour, cornmeal, baking powder, salt, and black pepper. Add the garlic powder, eggs and beer; mix well to combine.

In another shallow bowl, mix the breadcrumbs with the peanut oil. Dip the onion rings in the flour/egg mixture; then, dredge in the breadcrumb mixture. Roll to coat them evenly.

Spritz the Air Fryer basket with cooking spray; arrange the breaded onion rings in the basket.

Cook in the preheated Air Fryer at 400 degrees F for 4 to 5 minutes, turning them over halfway through the cooking time. Bon appétit!

Wonton Sausage Appetizers

(Ready in about 20 minutes | Servings 5)

Per serving: 199 Calories; 5.8g Fat; 19.2g Carbs; 14g Protein; 0.3g Sugars

Ingredients

1/2 pound ground sausage

2 tablespoons scallions, chopped

1 garlic clove, minced

1/2 tablespoon fish sauce

1 teaspoon Sriracha sauce

20 wonton wrappers

1 egg, whisked with 1 tablespoon water

Directions

In a mixing bowl, thoroughly combine the ground sausage, scallions, garlic, fish sauce, and Sriracha.

Divide the mixture between the wonton wrappers. Dip your fingers in the egg wash

Fold the wonton in half. Bring up the 2 ends of the wonton and use the egg wash to stick them together. Pinch the edges and coat each wonton with the egg wash.

Place the folded wontons in the lightly greased cooking basket. Cook at 360 degrees F for 10 minutes. Work in batches and serve warm. Bon appétit!

Cocktail Cranberry Meatballs

(Ready in about 15 minutes | Servings 5)

Per serving: 365 Calories; 11.6g Fat; 38.1g Carbs; 25.6g Protein; 28.4g Sugars

Ingredients

1/2 pound ground beef

1/2 pound ground turkey

1/4 cup Parmesan cheese, grated

1/4 cup breadcrumbs

1 small shallot, chopped

2 eggs, whisked

1/2 teaspoon garlic powder

1/2 teaspoon porcini powder

Sea salt and ground black pepper, to taste

1 teaspoon red pepper flakes, crushed

1 tablespoon soy sauce

1 (8-ounce) can jellied cranberry sauce

6 ounces tomato-based chili sauce

Directions

In a mixing bowl, combine the ground meat together with the cheese, breadcrumbs, shallot, eggs, and spices.

Shape the mixture into 1-inch balls.

Cook the meatballs in the preheated Air Fryer at 380 degrees for 5 minutes. Shake halfway through the cooking time. Work in batches.

Whisk the soy sauce, cranberry sauce, and chili sauce in a mixing bowl. Pour the sauce over the meatballs and bake an additional 2 minutes.

Serve with cocktail sticks. Bon appétit!

Paprika Potato Chips

(Ready in about 50 minutes | Servings 3)

Per serving: 190 Calories; 0.3g Fat; 43.8g Carbs; 4.7g Protein; 6.1g Sugars

Ingredients

3 potatoes, thinly sliced

1 teaspoon sea salt

1 teaspoon garlic powder

1 teaspoon paprika

1/4 cup ketchup

Directions

Add the sliced potatoes to a bowl with salted water. Let them soak for 30 minutes. Drain and rinse your potatoes.

Pat dry and toss with salt.

Cook in the preheated Air Fryer at 400 degrees F for 15 minutes, shaking the basket occasionally. Work in batches. Toss with the garlic powder and paprika. Serve with ketchup. Enjoy!

Barbecue Little Smokies

(Ready in about 20 minutes | Servings 6)

Per serving: 182 Calories; 4.6g Fat; 19.2g Carbs; 15.9g Protein; 15.7g Sugars

Ingredients

1 pound beef cocktail wieners

10 ounces barbecue sauce

Directions

Start by preheating your Air Fryer to 380 degrees F.

Prick holes into your sausages using a fork and transfer them to the baking pan.

Cook for 13 minutes. Spoon the barbecue sauce into the pan and cook an additional 2 minutes. Serve with toothpicks. Bon appétit!

Sweet Potato Fries with Spicy Dip

(Ready in about 50 minutes | Servings 3)

Per serving: 332 Calories; 23.6g Fat; 27.9g Carbs; 3g Protein; 9.8g Sugars

Ingredients

3 medium sweet potatoes, cut into 1/3-inch sticks

2 tablespoons olive oil

1 teaspoon kosher salt

Spicy Dip:

1/4 cup mayonnaise

1/4 cup Greek yogurt

1/4 teaspoon Dijon mustard

1 teaspoon hot sauce

Directions

Soak the sweet potato in icy cold water for 30 minutes. Drain the sweet potatoes and pat them dry with paper towels.

Toss the sweet potatoes with olive oil and salt.

Place in the lightly greased cooking basket. Cook in the preheated Air Fryer at 360 degrees F for 14 minutes. Wok in batches.

While the sweet potatoes are cooking, make the spicy dip by whisking the remaining ingredients. Place in the refrigerator until ready to serve. Enjoy!

Crunchy Broccoli Fries

(Ready in about 15 minutes | Servings 4)

Per serving: 127 Calories; 8.6g Fat; 9.9g Carbs; 4.9g Protein; 2.6g Sugars

Ingredients

1 pound broccoli florets

1/2 teaspoon onion powder

1 teaspoon granulated garlic

1/2 teaspoon cayenne pepper

Sea salt and ground black pepper, to taste
2 tablespoons sesame oil
4 tablespoons parmesan cheese, preferably freshly grated

Directions

Start by preheating the Air Fryer to 400 degrees F.

Blanch the broccoli in salted boiling water until al dente, about 3 to 4 minutes. Drain well and transfer to the lightly greased Air Fryer basket.

Add the onion powder, garlic, cayenne pepper, salt, black pepper, and sesame oil.

Cook for 6 minutes, tossing halfway through the cooking time. Bon appétit!

Kale Chips with Tahini Sauce

(Ready in about 15 minutes | Servings 4)
Per serving: 170 Calories; 15g Fat; 7.1g Carbs; 4.2g Protein; 0.7g Sugars

Ingredients

5 cups kale leaves, torn into 1-inch pieces
1 ½ tablespoons sesame oil
1/2 teaspoon shallot powder
1 teaspoon garlic powder
1/4 teaspoon porcini powder
1/2 teaspoon mustard seeds
1 teaspoon salt
1/3 cup tahini (sesame butter)
1 tablespoon fresh lemon juice
2 cloves garlic, minced

Directions

Toss the kale with the sesame oil and seasonings. Bake in the preheated Air Fryer at 350 degrees F for 10 minutes, shaking the cooking basket occasionally.

Bake until the edges are brown. Work in batches.

Meanwhile, make the sauce by whisking all ingredients in a small mixing bowl. Serve and enjoy!

Famous Blooming Onion with Mayo Dip

(Ready in about 25 minutes | Servings 3)
Per serving: 222 Calories; 9.9g Fat; 24.6g Carbs; 8.6g Protein; 3.9g Sugars

Ingredients

1 large Vidalia onion
1/2 cup all-purpose flour
1 teaspoon salt
1/2 teaspoon ground black pepper
1 teaspoon cayenne pepper
1/2 teaspoon dried thyme
1/2 teaspoon dried oregano
1/2 teaspoon ground cumin
2 eggs
1/4 cup milk
Mayo Dip:
3 tablespoons mayonnaise
3 tablespoons sour cream
1 tablespoon horseradish, drained
Kosher salt and freshly ground black pepper, to taste

Directions

Cut off the top 1/2 inch of the Vidalia onion; peel your onion and place it cut-side down. Starting 1/2 inch from the root, cut the onion in half. Make a second cut that splits each half in two. You will have 4 quarters held together by the root. Repeat these cuts, splitting the 4 quarters to yield eighths; then, you should split them again until you have 16 evenly spaced cuts. Turn the onion over and gently separate the outer pieces using your fingers.

In a mixing bowl, thoroughly combine the flour and spices. In a separate bowl, whisk the eggs and milk. Dip the onion into the egg mixture, followed by the flour mixture.

Spritz the onion with cooking spray and transfer to the lightly greased cooking basket. Cook for 370 degrees F for 12 to 15 minutes.

Meanwhile, make the mayo dip by whisking the remaining ingredients. Serve and enjoy!

Thyme-Roasted Sweet Potatoes

(Ready in about 35 minutes | Servings 3)
Per serving: 143 Calories; 9.7g Fat; 13.3g Carbs; 3.7g Protein; 0g Sugars

Ingredients

1 pound sweet potatoes, peeled, cut into bite-sized pieces
2 tablespoons olive oil
1 teaspoon sea salt
1/4 teaspoon freshly ground black pepper
1/2 teaspoon cayenne pepper
2 fresh thyme sprigs

Directions

Arrange the potato slices in a single layer in the lightly greased cooking basket. Add the olive oil, salt, black pepper, and cayenne pepper; toss to coat.

Bake at 380 degrees F for 30 minutes, shaking the cooking basket occasionally.

Bake until tender and slightly browned, working in batches. Serve warm, garnished with thyme sprigs. Bon appétit!

Chicken Nuggets with Campfire Sauce

(Ready in about 20 minutes | Servings 6)

Per serving: 211 Calories; 5.4g Fat; 18.4g Carbs; 18.9g Protein; 6.3g Sugars

Ingredients

1 pound chicken breasts, slice into tenders
1/2 teaspoon cayenne pepper
Salt and black pepper, to taste
1/4 cup cornmeal
1 egg, whisked
1/2 cup seasoned breadcrumbs
1/4 cup mayo
1/4 cup barbecue sauce

Directions

Pat the chicken tenders dry with a kitchen towel. Season with the cayenne pepper, salt, and black pepper.

Dip the chicken tenders into the cornmeal, followed by the egg. Press the chicken tenders into the breadcrumbs, coating evenly.

Place the chicken tenders in the lightly greased Air Fryer basket. Cook at 360 degrees for 9 to 12 minutes, turning them over to cook evenly.

In a mixing bowl, thoroughly combine the mayonnaise with the barbecue sauce. Serve the chicken nuggets with the sauce for dipping. Bon appétit!

Avocado Fries with Chipotle Sauce

(Ready in about 20 minutes | Servings 3)
Per serving: 273 Calories; 18.4g Fat; 23.1g Carbs; 6.7g Protein; 7.7g Sugars

Ingredients

2 tablespoons fresh lime juice
1 avocado, pitted, peeled, and sliced
Pink Himalayan salt and ground white pepper, to taste
1/4 cup flour

1 egg

1/2 cup breadcrumbs

1 chipotle chili in adobo sauce

1/4 cup light mayonnaise

1/4 cup plain Greek yogurt

Directions

Drizzle lime juice all over the avocado slices and set aside.

Then, set up your breading station. Mix the salt, pepper, and all-purpose flour in a shallow dish. In a separate dish, whisk the egg.

Finally, place your breadcrumbs in a third dish.

Start by dredging the avocado slices in the flour mixture; then, dip them into the egg. Press the avocado slices into the breadcrumbs, coating evenly.

Cook in the preheating Air Fryer at 380 degrees F for 11 minutes, shaking the cooking basket halfway through the cooking time.

Meanwhile, blend the chipotle chili, mayo, and Greek yogurt in your food processor until the sauce is creamy and uniform.

Serve the warm avocado slices with the sauce on the side. Enjoy!

Asian Twist Chicken Wings

(Ready in about 20 minutes | Servings 6)

Per serving: 195 Calories; 5.7g Fat; 9.4g Carbs; 25.5g Protein; 6.4g Sugars

Ingredients

1 ½ pounds chicken wings

2 teaspoons sesame oil

Kosher salt and ground black pepper, to taste

2 tablespoons tamari sauce

1 tablespoon rice vinegar

2 garlic clove, minced

2 tablespoons honey

2 sun-dried tomatoes, minced

Directions

Toss the chicken wings with the sesame oil, salt, and pepper. Add chicken wings to a lightly greased baking pan.

Roast the chicken wings in the preheated Air Fryer at 390 degrees F for 7 minutes. Turn them over once or twice to ensure even cooking.

In a mixing dish, thoroughly combine the tamari sauce, vinegar, garlic, honey, and sun-dried tomatoes.

Pour the sauce all over the chicken wings; bake an additional 5 minutes. Bon appétit!

Roasted Cauliflower Florets

(Ready in about 20 minutes | Servings 2)

Per serving: 80 Calories; 4.9g Fat; 7.9g Carbs; 3.1g Protein; 3.1g Sugars

Ingredients

3 cups cauliflower florets

2 teaspoons sesame oil

1 teaspoon onion powder

1 teaspoon garlic powder

Sea salt and cracked black pepper, to taste

1 teaspoon paprika

Directions

Start by preheating your Air Fryer to 400 degrees F.

Toss the cauliflower with the remaining ingredients; toss to coat well.

Cook for 12 minutes, shaking the cooking basket halfway through the cooking time. They will crisp up as they cool. Bon appétit!

Parsnip Chips with Spicy Citrus Aioli

(Ready in about 20 minutes | Servings 4)

Per serving: 207 Calories; 12.1g Fat; 23.8g Carbs; 2.8g Protein; 7g Sugars

Ingredients

1 pound parsnips, peel long strips

2 tablespoons sesame oil

Sea salt and ground black pepper, to taste

1 teaspoon red pepper flakes, crushed

1/2 teaspoon curry powder

1/2 teaspoon mustard seeds

Spicy Citrus Aioli:

1/4 cup mayonnaise

1 tablespoon fresh lime juice

1 clove garlic, smashed

Salt and black pepper, to taste

Directions

Start by preheating the Air Fryer to 380 degrees F.

Toss the parsnip chips with the sesame oil, salt, black pepper, red pepper, curry powder, and mustard seeds.

Cook for 15 minutes, shaking the Air Fryer basket periodically.

Meanwhile, make the sauce by whisking the mayonnaise, lime juice, garlic, salt, and pepper. Place in the refrigerator until ready to use. Bon appétit!

Classic Deviled Eggs

(Ready in about 20 minutes | Servings 3)

Per serving: 261 Calories; 19.2g Fat; 5.5g Carbs; 15.5g Protein; 4.1g Sugars

Ingredients

5 eggs

2 tablespoons mayonnaise

2 tablespoons sweet pickle relish

Sea salt, to taste

1/2 teaspoon mixed peppercorns, crushed

Directions

Place the wire rack in the Air Fryer basket; lower the eggs onto the wire rack.

Cook at 270 degrees F for 15 minutes.

Transfer them to an ice-cold water bath to stop the cooking. Peel the eggs under cold running water; slice them into halves.

Mash the egg yolks with the mayo, sweet pickle relish, and salt; spoon yolk mixture into egg whites. Arrange on a nice serving platter and garnish with the mixed peppercorns. Bon appétit!

Cajun Cheese Sticks

(Ready in about 15 minutes | Servings 4)

Per serving: 372 Calories; 22.7g Fat; 19.5g Carbs; 21.8g Protein; 3.8g Sugars

Ingredients

1/2 cup all-purpose flour

2 eggs

1/2 cup parmesan cheese, grated

1 tablespoon Cajun seasonings

8 cheese sticks, kid-friendly

1/4 cup ketchup

Directions

To begin, set up your breading station. Place the all-purpose flour in a shallow dish. In a separate dish, whisk the eggs.

Finally, mix the parmesan cheese and Cajun seasoning in a third dish.

Start by dredging the cheese sticks in the flour; then, dip them into the egg. Press the cheese sticks into the parmesan mixture, coating evenly. Place the breaded cheese sticks in the lightly greased Air Fryer basket. Cook at 380 degrees F for 6 minutes.

Serve with ketchup and enjoy!

Puerto Rican Tostones

(Ready in about 15 minutes | Servings 2)

Per serving: 151 Calories; 7.1g Fat; 23.9g Carbs; 0.6g Protein; 10.7g Sugars

Ingredients

1 ripe plantain, sliced
1 tablespoon sunflower oil
A pinch of grated nutmeg
A pinch of kosher salt

Directions

Toss the plantains with the oil, nutmeg, and salt in a bowl.

Cook in the preheated Air Fryer at 400 degrees F for 10 minutes, shaking the cooking basket halfway through the cooking time.

Adjust the seasonings to taste and serve immediately.

The Best Calamari Appetizer

(Ready in about 20 minutes | Servings 6)

Per serving: 274 Calories; 3.3g Fat; 36.8g Carbs; 22.9g Protein; 1.3g Sugars

Ingredients

1 ½ pounds calamari tubes, cleaned, cut into rings
Sea salt and ground black pepper, to taste
2 tablespoons lemon juice
1 cup cornmeal
1 cup all-purpose flour
1 teaspoon paprika
1 egg, whisked
1/4 cup buttermilk

Directions

Preheat your Air Fryer to 390 degrees F. Rinse the calamari and pat it dry. Season with salt and black pepper. Drizzle lemon juice all over the calamari.

Now, combine the cornmeal, flour, and paprika in a bowl; add the whisked egg and buttermilk. Dredge the calamari in the egg/flour mixture. Arrange them in the cooking basket. Spritz with cooking oil and cook for 9 to 12 minutes, shaking the basket occasionally. Work in batches.
Serve with toothpicks. Bon appétit!

Fried Pickle Chips with Greek Yogurt Dip

(Ready in about 20 minutes | Servings 5)

Per serving: 138 Calories; 3.2g Fat; 21.8g Carbs; 5.7g Protein; 1.9g Sugars

Ingredients

1/2 cup cornmeal
1/2 cup all-purpose flour
1 teaspoon cayenne pepper
1/2 teaspoon shallot powder
1 teaspoon garlic powder
1/2 teaspoon porcini powder
Kosher salt and ground black pepper, to taste
2 eggs
2 cups pickle chips, pat dry with kitchen towels
Greek Yogurt Dip:
1/2 cup Greek yogurt
1 clove garlic, minced
1/4 teaspoon ground black pepper
1 tablespoon fresh chives, chopped

Directions

In a shallow bowl, mix the cornmeal and flour; add the seasonings and mix to combine well. Beat the eggs in a separate shallow bowl.

Dredge the pickle chips in the flour mixture, then, in the egg mixture. Press the pickle chips into the flour mixture again, coating evenly.

Cook in the preheated Air Fryer at 400 degrees F for 5 minutes; shake the basket and cook for 5 minutes more. Work in batches.

Meanwhile, mix all the sauce ingredients until well combined. Serve the fried pickles with the Greek yogurt dip and enjoy.

Teriyaki Chicken Drumettes

(Ready in about 40 minutes | Servings 6)

Per serving: 286 Calories; 14.8g Fat; 13.5g Carbs; 23.8g Protein; 12.1g Sugars

Ingredients

1 ½ pounds chicken drumettes
Sea salt and cracked black pepper, to taste
2 tablespoons fresh chives, roughly chopped
Teriyaki Sauce:
1 tablespoon sesame oil
1/4 cup soy sauce
1/2 cup water
1/4 cup honey
1/2 teaspoon Five-spice powder
2 tablespoons rice wine vinegar
1/2 teaspoon fresh ginger, grated
2 cloves garlic, crushed
1 tablespoon corn starch dissolved in 3 tablespoons of water

Directions

Start by preheating your Air Fryer to 380 degrees F. Rub the chicken drumettes with salt and cracked black pepper.

Cook in the preheated Air Fryer approximately 15 minutes. Turn them over and cook an additional 7 minutes.

While the chicken drumettes are roasting, combine the sesame oil, soy sauce, water, honey, Five-spice powder, vinegar, ginger, and garlic in a pan over medium heat. Cook for 5 minutes, stirring occasionally.

Add the cornstarch slurry, reduce the heat, and let it simmer until the glaze thickens.

After that, brush the glaze all over the chicken drumettes. Air-fry for a further 6 minutes or until the surface is crispy. Serve topped with the remaining glaze and garnished with fresh chives. Bon appétit!

Baked Cheese Crisps

(Ready in about 15 minutes | Servings 4)

Per serving: 198 Calories; 14.7g Fat; 4.7g Carbs; 12g Protein; 1.4g Sugars

Ingredients

1/2 cup Parmesan cheese, shredded
1 cup Cheddar cheese, shredded
1 teaspoon Italian seasoning
1/2 cup marinara sauce

Directions

Start by preheating your Air Fryer to 350 degrees F. Place a piece of parchment paper in the cooking basket.

Mix the cheese with the Italian seasoning.

Add about 1 tablespoon of the cheese mixture (per crisp) to the basket, making sure they are not touching. Bake for 6 minutes or until browned to your liking.

Work in batches and place them on a large tray to cool slightly. Serve with the marinara sauce. Bon appétit!

Mexican Cheesy Zucchini Bites

(Ready in about 25 minutes | Servings 4)

Per serving: 231 Calories; 9g Fat; 29.3g Carbs; 8.4g Protein; 2.3g Sugars

Ingredients

1 large-sized zucchini, thinly sliced

1/2 cup flour

1/4 cup yellow cornmeal

1 egg, whisked

1/2 cup tortilla chips, crushed

1/2 cup Queso Añejo, grated

Salt and cracked pepper, to taste

Directions

Pat dry the zucchini slices with a kitchen towel. Mix the remaining ingredients in a shallow bowl; mix until everything is well combined. Dip each zucchini slice in the prepared batter.

Cook in the preheated Air Fryer at 400 degrees F for 12 minutes, shaking the basket halfway through the cooking time.

Work in batches until the zucchini slices are crispy and golden brown. Enjoy!

Bruschetta with Fresh Tomato and Basil

(Ready in about 15 minutes | Servings 3)

Per serving: 161 Calories; 5.5g Fat; 23.8g Carbs; 4.4g Protein; 4.5g Sugars

Ingredients

1/2 Italian bread, sliced

2 garlic cloves, peeled

2 tablespoons extra-virgin olive oil

2 ripe tomatoes, chopped

1 teaspoon dried oregano

Salt, to taste

8 fresh basil leaves, roughly chopped

Directions

Place the bread slices on the lightly greased Air Fryer grill pan. Bake at 370 degrees F for 3 minutes.

Cut a clove of garlic in half and rub over one side of the toast; brush with olive oil. Add the chopped tomatoes. Sprinkle with oregano and salt.

Increase the temperature to 380 degrees F. Cook in the preheated Air Fryer for 3 minutes more. Garnish with fresh basil and serve. Bon appétit!

Roasted Parsnip Sticks with Salted Caramel

(Ready in about 25 minutes | Servings 4)

Per serving: 213 Calories; 13.1g Fat; 24.4g Carbs; 1.4g Protein; 9.3g Sugars

Ingredients

1 pound parsnip, trimmed, scrubbed, cut into sticks

2 tablespoon avocado oil

2 tablespoons granulated sugar

2 tablespoons butter

1/4 teaspoon ground allspice

1/2 teaspoon coarse salt

Directions

Toss the parsnip with the avocado oil; bake in the preheated Air Fryer at 380 degrees F for 15 minutes, shaking the cooking basket occasionally to ensure even cooking.

Then, heat the sugar and 1 tablespoon of water in a small pan over medium heat. Cook until the sugar has dissolved; bring to a boil.

Keep swirling the pan around until the sugar reaches a rich caramel color. Pour in 2 tablespoons of cold water. Now, add the butter, allspice, and salt. The mixture should be runny.

Afterwards, drizzle the salted caramel over the roasted parsnip sticks and enjoy!

Greek-Style Squash Chips

(Ready in about 25 minutes | Servings 4)

Per serving: 180 Calories; 10.3g Fat; 13.3g Carbs; 5.8g Protein; 2.8g Sugars

Ingredients

1/2 cup seasoned breadcrumbs

1/2 cup Parmesan cheese, grated

Sea salt and ground black pepper, to taste

1/4 teaspoon oregano

2 yellow squash, cut into slices

2 tablespoons grapeseed oil

Sauce:

1/2 cup Greek-style yogurt

1 tablespoon fresh cilantro, chopped

1 garlic clove, minced

Freshly ground black pepper, to your liking

Directions

In a shallow bowl, thoroughly combine the seasoned breadcrumbs, Parmesan, salt, black pepper, and oregano.

Dip the yellow squash slices in the prepared batter, pressing to adhere.

Brush with the grapeseed oil and cook in the preheated Air Fryer at 400 degrees F for 12 minutes. Shake the Air Fryer basket periodically to ensure even cooking. Work in batches.

While the chips are baking, whisk the sauce ingredients; place in your refrigerator until ready to serve. Enjoy!

RICE & GRAINS

Cinnamon Breakfast Muffins

(Ready in about 20 minutes | Servings 4)

Per serving: 302 Calories; 17.1g Fat; 27.7g Carbs; 8.3g Protein; 3.3g Sugars

Ingredients

1 cup all-purpose flour

1 teaspoon baking powder

1 tablespoon brown sugar

2 eggs

1 teaspoon cinnamon powder

1 teaspoon vanilla paste

1/4 cup milk

4 tablespoons butter, melted

Directions

Start by preheating your Air Fryer to 330 degrees F. Now, spritz the silicone muffin tins with cooking spray.

Thoroughly combine all ingredients in a mixing dish. Fill the muffin cups with batter.

Cook in the preheated Air Fryer approximately 13 minutes. Check with a toothpick; when the toothpick comes out clean, your muffins are done. Place on a rack to cool slightly before removing from the muffin tins. Enjoy!

Hibachi-Style Fried Rice

(Ready in about 30 minutes | Servings 2)

Per serving: 428 Calories; 13.4g Fat; 58.9g Carbs; 14.4g Protein; 4.7g Sugars

Ingredients

1 ¾ cups leftover jasmine rice

2 teaspoons butter, melted

Sea salt and freshly ground black pepper, to your liking

2 eggs, beaten

2 scallions, white and green parts separated, chopped

1 cup snow peas

1 tablespoon Shoyu sauce

1 tablespoon sake

2 tablespoons Kewpie Japanese mayonnaise

Directions

Thoroughly combine the rice, butter, salt, and pepper in a baking dish.

Cook at 340 degrees F about 13 minutes, stirring halfway through the cooking time.

Pour the eggs over the rice and continue to cook about 5 minutes. Next, add the scallions and snow peas and stir to combine. Continue to cook 2 to 3 minutes longer or until everything is heated through.

Meanwhile, make the sauce by whisking the Shoyu sauce, sake, and Japanese mayonnaise in a mixing bowl.

Divide the fried rice between individual bowls and serve with the prepared sauce. Enjoy!

Italian Panettone Bread Pudding

(Ready in about 45 minutes | Servings 3)

Per serving: 279 Calories; 8.7g Fat; 37.9g Carbs; 8.9g Protein; 23.1g Sugars

Ingredients

4 slices of panettone bread, crusts trimmed, bread cut into 1-inch cubes

4 tablespoons dried cranberries

2 tablespoons amaretto liqueur

1 cup coconut milk

1/2 cup whipping cream

2 eggs

1 tablespoon agave syrup

1/2 vanilla extract

1/2 teaspoon ground cloves

1/2 teaspoon ground cinnamon

Directions

Place the panettone bread cubes in a lightly greased baking dish. Scatter the dried cranberry over the top. In a mixing bowl, thoroughly combine the remaining ingredients.

Pour the custard over the bread cubes. Let it stand for 30 minutes, occasionally pressing with a wide spatula to submerge.

Cook in the preheated Air Fryer at 370 degrees F degrees for 7 minutes; check to ensure even cooking and cook an additional 5 to 6 minutes. Bon appétit!

Classic Italian Arancini

(Ready in about 35 minutes | Servings 2)

Per serving: 348 Calories; 7.5g Fat; 52.2g Carbs; 15.8g Protein; 2.4g Sugars

Ingredients

1 ½ cups chicken broth

1/2 cup white rice

2 tablespoons parmesan cheese, grated

Sea salt and cracked black pepper, to your liking

2 eggs

1 cup fresh bread crumbs

1/2 teaspoon oregano

1 teaspoon basil

Directions

Bring the chicken broth to a boil in a saucepan over medium-high heat. Stir in the rice and reduce the heat to simmer; cook about 20 minutes. Drain the rice and allow it to cool completely.

Add the parmesan, salt, and black pepper. Shape the mixture into bite-sized balls.

In a shallow bowl, beat the eggs; in another shallow bowl, mix bread crumbs with oregano and basil.

Dip each rice ball into the beaten eggs, then, roll in the breadcrumb mixture, gently pressing to adhere.

Bake in the preheated Air Fryer at 350 degrees F for 10 to 12 minutes, flipping them halfway through the cooking time. Bon appétit!

Smoked Salmon and Rice Rollups

(Ready in about 25 minutes | Servings 3)

Per serving: 226 Calories; 11.6g Fat; 15.1g Carbs; 15.2g Protein; 1.9g Sugars

Ingredients

1 tablespoon fresh lemon juice

6 slices smoked salmon

1 tablespoon extra-virgin olive oil

1/2 cup cooked rice

1 tablespoon whole-grain mustard

3 tablespoons shallots, chopped

1 garlic clove, minced

1 teaspoon capers, rinsed and chopped

Sea salt and ground black pepper, to taste

3 ounces sour cream

Directions

Drizzle the lemon juice all over the smoked salmon.

Then, spread each salmon strip with olive oil. In a mixing bowl, thoroughly combine the cooked rice, mustard, shallots, garlic, and capers.

Spread the rice mixture over the olive oil. Roll the slices into individual rollups and secure with a toothpick. Season with salt and black pepper.

Place in the lightly greased Air Fryer basket. Bake at 370 degrees F for 16 minutes, turning them over halfway through the cooking time. Serve with sour cream and enjoy!

Spicy Seafood Risotto

(Ready in about 25 minutes | Servings 3)

Per serving: 445 Calories; 17.7g Fat; 48.8g Carbs; 24.4g Protein; 2.5g Sugars

Ingredients

1 ½ cups cooked rice, cold

3 tablespoons shallots, minced

2 garlic cloves, minced

1 tablespoon oyster sauce

2 tablespoons dry white wine

2 tablespoons sesame oil

Salt and ground black pepper, to taste

2 eggs

4 ounces lump crab meat

1 teaspoon ancho chili powder

2 tablespoons fresh parsley, roughly chopped

Directions

Mix the cold rice, shallots, garlic, oyster sauce, dry white wine, sesame oil, salt, and black pepper in a lightly greased baking pan. Stir in the whisked eggs.

Cook in the preheated Air Fryer at 370 degrees for 13 to 16 minutes.

Add the crab and ancho chili powder to the baking dish; stir until everything is well combined. Cook for 6 minutes more.

Serve at room temperature, garnished with fresh parsley. Bon appétit!

Polenta Fries with Sriracha Sauce

(Ready in about 45 minutes + chilling time | Servings 3)

Per serving: 247 Calories; 6.5g Fat; 43.8g Carbs; 3.7g Protein; 11.5g Sugars

Ingredients

Polenta Fries:

1 ½ cups water

1 teaspoon sea salt

1/2 cup polenta

1 tablespoon butter, room temperature

A pinch of grated nutmeg

1 teaspoon dried Italian herb mix

Sriracha Sauce:

1 red jalapeno pepper, minced

1 garlic clove, minced

1 tablespoon cider vinegar

2 tablespoons tomato paste

1 tablespoon honey

Directions

Bring the water and 1 teaspoon sea salt to a boil in a saucepan; slowly and gradually stir in the polenta, whisking continuously until there are no lumps.

Reduce the heat to simmer and cook for 5 to 6 minutes until the polenta starts to thicken. Cover and continue to simmer for 25 minutes or until you have a thick mixture, whisking periodically. Stir in the butter, nutmeg, and Italian herbs.

Pour your polenta into a parchment-lined rimmed baking tray, spreading the mixture evenly. Cover with plastic wrap; let it stand in your refrigerator for about 2 hours to firm up.

Then, slice the polenta into strips and place them in the greased Air Fryer basket. Cook in the preheated Air Fryer at 395 degrees F for about 11 minutes.

Meanwhile, make the Sriracha sauce by whisking all ingredients. Serve the warm polenta fries with the Sriracha sauce on the side. Enjoy!

Basic Air Fryer Granola

(Ready in about 45 minutes | Servings 12)

Per serving: 103 Calories; 6.8g Fat; 8.8g Carbs; 3.1g Protein; 3.1g Sugars

Ingredients

1/2 cup rolled oats

1 cup walnuts, chopped

3 tablespoons sunflower seeds

3 tablespoons pumpkin seeds

1 teaspoon coarse sea salt

2 tablespoons honey

Directions

Thoroughly combine all ingredients and spread the mixture onto the Air Fryer trays. Spritz with nonstick cooking spray.

Bake at 230 degrees F for 25 minutes; rotate the trays and bake 10 to 15 minutes more.

This granola can be kept in an airtight container for up to 2 weeks. Enjoy!

Taco Stuffed Bread

(Ready in about 15 minutes | Servings 4)

Per serving: 472 Calories; 21.9g Fat; 37.6g Carbs; 30.5g Protein; 6.6g Sugars

Ingredients

1 loaf French bread

1/2 pound ground beef

1 onion, chopped

1 teaspoon garlic, minced

1 package taco seasoning

1 ½ cups Queso Panela, sliced

Salt and ground black pepper, to taste

3 tablespoons tomato paste

2 tablespoons fresh cilantro leaves, chopped

Directions

Cut the top off of the loaf of bread; remove some of the bread from the middle creating a well and reserve.

In a large skillet, cook the ground beef with the onion and garlic until the beef is no longer pink and the onion is translucent.

Add the taco seasoning, cheese, salt, black pepper, and tomato paste. Place the taco mixture into your bread.

Bake in the preheated Air Fryer at 380 degrees F for 5 minutes. Garnish with fresh cilantro leaves. Enjoy!

New York-Style Pizza

(Ready in about 15 minutes | Servings 4)

Per serving: 308 Calories; 4.1g Fat; 25.7g Carbs; 42.7g Protein; 6.1g Sugars

Ingredients

1 pizza dough

1 cup tomato sauce

14 ounces mozzarella cheese, freshly grated

2 ounces parmesan, freshly grated

Directions

Stretch your dough on a pizza peel lightly dusted with flour. Spread with a layer of tomato sauce. Top with cheese. Place on the baking tray.

Bake in the preheated Air Fryer at 395 degrees F for 5 minutes. Rotate the baking tray and bake for a further 5 minutes. Serve immediately.

Favorite Cheese Biscuits

(Ready in about 30 minutes | Servings 4)

Per serving: 462 Calories; 25.8g Fat; 39.1g Carbs; 17.6g Protein; 2.1g Sugars

Ingredients

1 ½ cups all-purpose flour
1/3 cup butter, room temperature
1 teaspoon baking powder
1 teaspoon baking soda
1/2 cup buttermilk
2 eggs, beaten
1 cup Swiss cheese, shredded

Directions

In a mixing bowl, thoroughly combine the flour and butter. Gradually stir in the remaining ingredients.

Divide the mixture into 12 balls.

Bake in the preheated Air Fryer at 360 degrees F for 15 minutes. Work in two batches.

Serve at room temperature. Bon appétit!

Pretzel Knots with Cumin Seeds

(Ready in about 25 minutes | Servings 6)

Per serving: 121 Calories; 6.5g Fat; 11.1g Carbs; 3.9g Protein; 3.1g Sugars

Ingredients

1 package crescent refrigerator rolls
2 eggs, whisked with 4 tablespoons of water
1 teaspoon cumin seeds

Directions

Roll the dough out into a rectangle. Slice the dough into 6 pieces.

Roll each piece into a log and tie each rope into a knot. Cover and let it rest for 10 minutes.

Brush the top of the pretzel knots with the egg wash; sprinkle with the cumin seeds. Arrange the pretzel knots in the lightly greased Air Fryer basket.

Bake in the preheated Air Fryer at 340 degrees for 7 minutes until golden brown. Bon appétit!

Delicious Turkey Sammies

(Ready in about 50 minutes | Servings 4)

Per serving: 452 Calories; 24.8g Fat; 22.9g Carbs; 38.5g Protein; 9.1g Sugars

Ingredients

1/2 pound turkey tenderloins
1 tablespoon olive oil
Salt and ground black pepper, to your liking
4 slices bread
1/4 cup tomato paste
1/4 cup pesto sauce
1 yellow onion, thinly sliced
1 cup mozzarella cheese, shredded

Directions

Brush the turkey tenderloins with olive oil. Season with salt and black pepper.

Cook the turkey tenderloins at 350 degrees F for 30 minutes, flipping them over halfway through. Let them rest for 5 to 9 minutes before slicing.

Cut the turkey tenderloins into thin slices. Make your sandwiches with bread, tomato paste, pesto, and onion. Place the turkey slices on top. Add the cheese and place the sandwiches in the Air Fryer basket.

Then, preheat your Air Fryer to 390 degrees F. Bake for 7 minutes or until cheese is melted. Serve immediately.

Mexican-Style Brown Rice Casserole

(Ready in about 50 minutes | Servings 4)

Per serving: 433 Calories; 7.4g Fat; 79.6g Carbs; 12.1g Protein; 2.8g Sugars

Ingredients

1 tablespoon olive oil
1 shallot, chopped
2 cloves garlic, minced
1 habanero pepper, minced
2 cups brown rice
3 cups chicken broth
1 cup water
2 ripe tomatoes, pureed
Sea salt and ground black pepper, to taste
1/2 teaspoon dried Mexican oregano
1 teaspoon red pepper flakes
1 cup Mexican Cotija cheese, crumbled

Directions

In a nonstick skillet, heat the olive oil over a moderate flame. Once hot, cook the shallot, garlic, and habanero pepper until tender and fragrant; reserve.

Heat the brown rice, vegetable broth and water in a pot over high heat. Bring it to a boil; turn the stove down to simmer and cook for 35 minutes.

Grease a baking pan with nonstick cooking spray. Spoon the cooked rice into the baking pan. Add the sautéed mixture. Spoon the tomato puree over the sautéed mixture. Sprinkle with salt, black pepper, oregano, and red pepper.

Cook in the preheated Air Fryer at 380 degrees F for 8 minutes. Top with the Cotija cheese and bake for 5 minutes longer or until cheese is melted. Enjoy!

Japanese Chicken and Rice Salad

(Ready in about 45 minutes + chilling time | Servings 4)

Per serving: 387 Calories; 4.7g Fat; 63.9g Carbs; 22.4g Protein; 3.9g Sugars

Ingredients

1 pound chicken tenderloins
2 tablespoons shallots, chopped
1 garlic clove, minced
1 red bell pepper, chopped
1 ½ cups brown rice
1 cup baby spinach
1/2 cup snow peas
2 tablespoons soy sauce
1 teaspoon yellow mustard
1 tablespoon rice vinegar
1 tablespoon liquid from pickled ginger
1 teaspoon agave syrup
2 tablespoons black sesame seeds, to serve
1/4 cup Mandarin orange segments

Directions

Start by preheating your Air Fryer to 380 degrees F. Then, add the chicken tenderloins to the baking pan and cook until it starts to get crisp or about 6 minutes.

Add the shallots, garlic, and bell pepper. Cook for 6 minutes more. Wait for the chicken mixture to cool down completely and transfer to a salad bowl.

Bring 3 cups of water and 1 teaspoon of salt to a boil in a saucepan over medium-high heat. Stir in the rice and reduce the heat to simmer; cook about 20 minutes.

Let your rice sit in the covered saucepan for another 10 minutes. Drain the rice and allow it to cool completely.

Stir the cold rice into the salad bowl; add the baby spinach and snow peas. In a small mixing dish, whisk the soy sauce, mustard, rice vinegar, liquid from pickled ginger, and agave syrup. Dress the salad and stir well to combine. Garnish with black sesame seeds and Mandarin orange. Enjoy!

Risotto Balls with Bacon and Corn

(Ready in about 30 minutes + chilling time | Servings 6)

Per serving: 435 Calories; 15.6g Fat; 47.4g Carbs; 23.3g Protein; 4.1g Sugars

Ingredients

4 slices Canadian bacon

1 tablespoon olive oil

1/2 medium-sized leek, chopped

1 teaspoon fresh garlic, minced

Sea salt and freshly ground pepper, to taste

1 cup white rice

4 cups vegetable broth

1/3 cup dry white wine

2 tablespoons tamari sauce

1 tablespoon oyster sauce

1 tablespoon butter

1 cup sweet corn kernels

1 bell pepper, seeded and chopped

2 eggs lightly beaten

1 cup bread crumbs

1 cup parmesan cheese, preferably freshly grated

Directions

Cook the Canadian bacon in a nonstick skillet over medium-high heat. Let it cool, finely chop and reserve.

Heat the olive oil in a saucepan over medium heat. Now, sauté the leeks and garlic, stirring occasionally, about 5 minutes. Add the salt and pepper.

Stir in the white rice. Continue to cook approximately 3 minutes or until translucent. Add the warm broth, wine, tamari sauce, and oyster sauce; cook until the liquid is absorbed.

Remove the saucepan from the heat; stir in the butter, corn, bell pepper, and reserved Canadian bacon. Let it cool completely. Then, shape the mixture into small balls.

In a shallow bowl, combine the eggs with the breadcrumbs and parmesan cheese. Dip each ball in the eggs/crumb mixture.

Cook in the preheated Air Fryer at 395 degrees F for 10 to 12 minutes, shaking the basket periodically. Serve warm.

Ciabatta Bread Pudding with Walnuts

(Ready in about 45 minutes | Servings 4)

Per serving: 454 Calories; 18.2g Fat; 56.7g Carbs; 18.3g Protein; 25.1g Sugars

Ingredients

4 cups ciabatta bread cubes

2 eggs, slightly beaten

1 cup milk

2 tablespoons butter

4 tablespoons honey

1 teaspoon vanilla extract

1/2 teaspoon ground cloves

1/2 teaspoon ground cinnamon

A pinch of salt

A pinch of grated nutmeg

1/3 cup walnuts, chopped

Directions

Place the ciabatta bread cubes in a lightly greased baking dish. In a mixing bowl, thoroughly combine the eggs, milk, butter, honey, vanilla, ground cloves, cinnamon, salt, and nutmeg.

Pour the custard over the bread cubes. Scatter the chopped walnuts over the top of your bread pudding.

Let stand for 30 minutes, occasionally pressing with a wide spatula to submerge.

Cook in the preheated Air Fryer at 370 degrees F degrees for 7 minutes; check to ensure even cooking and cook an additional 5 to 6 minutes. Bon appétit!

Sunday Glazed Cinnamon Rolls

(Ready in about 15 minutes | Servings 4)
Per serving: 313 Calories; 10.8g Fat; 52.9g Carbs; 2.1g Protein; 39.4g Sugars

Ingredients
1 can cinnamon rolls
2 tablespoons butter
1 cup powdered sugar
1 teaspoon vanilla extract
3 tablespoons hot water

Directions
Place the cinnamon rolls in the Air Fryer basket. Bake at 300 degrees F for 10 minutes, flipping them halfway through the cooking time.

Meanwhile, mix the butter, sugar, and vanilla. Pour in water, 1 tablespoon at a time, until the glaze reaches desired consistency.

Spread over the slightly cooled cinnamon rolls. Bon appétit!

Rich Couscous Salad with Goat Cheese

(Ready in about 45 minutes | Servings 4)
Per serving: 258 Calories; 13g Fat; 28.3g Carbs; 8.8g Protein; 8.2g Sugars

Ingredients
1/2 cup couscous

4 teaspoons olive oil
1/2 lemon, juiced, zested
1 tablespoon honey
Sea salt and freshly ground black pepper, to your liking
2 tomatoes, sliced
1 red onion, thinly sliced
1/2 English cucumber, thinly sliced
2 ounces goat cheese, crumbled
1 teaspoon ghee
2 tablespoons pine nuts
1/2 cup loosely packed Italian parsley, finely chopped

Directions
Put the couscous in a bowl; now, pour the boiling water over it. Cover and set aside for 5 to 8 minutes; fluff with a fork.

Place the couscous in a cake pan. Transfer the pan to the Air Fryer basket and cook at 360 digress F about 20 minutes. Make sure to stir every 5 minutes to ensure even cooking.

Meanwhile, in a small mixing bowl, whisk the olive oil, lemon juice and zest, honey, salt, and black pepper. Toss the couscous with this dressing.

Add the tomatoes, red onion, English cucumber, and goat cheese; gently stir to combine.

Rub the ghee in the pine nuts, using your hands and place them in the Air Fryer basket. Roast for 4 minutes; give the nuts a good toss. Put the cooking basket back again and roast for a further 3 to 4 minutes.

Scatter the toasted nuts over your salad and garnish with parsley. Enjoy!

The Best Fish Tacos Ever

(Ready in about 25 minutes | Servings 3)
Per serving: 493 Calories; 19.2g Fat; 48.4g Carbs; 30.8g Protein; 5.8g Sugars

Ingredients

1 tablespoon mayonnaise
1 teaspoon Dijon mustard
1 tablespoon sour cream
1/2 teaspoon fresh garlic, minced
1/4 teaspoon red pepper flakes
Sea salt, to taste
2 bell peppers, seeded and sliced
1 shallot, thinly sliced
1 egg
1 tablespoon water
1 tablespoon taco seasoning mix
1/3 cup tortilla chips, crushed
1/4 cup parmesan cheese, grated
1 halibut fillets, cut into 1-inch strips
6 mini flour taco shells
6 lime wedges, for serving

Directions

Thoroughly combine the mayonnaise, mustard, sour cream, garlic, red pepper flakes, and salt. Add the bell peppers and shallots; toss to coat well. Place in your refrigerator until ready to serve. Line the Air Fryer basket with a piece of parchment paper.

In a shallow bowl, mix the egg, water, and taco seasoning mix. In a separate shallow bowl, mix the crushed tortilla chips and parmesan.

Dip the fish into the egg mixture, then coat with the parmesan mixture, pressing to adhere.

Bake in the preheated Air Fryer at 380 degrees F for 13 minutes, flipping halfway through the cooking time.

Divide the creamed pepper mixture among the taco shells. Top with the fish, and serve with lime wedges. Enjoy!

Savory Cheese and Herb Biscuits

(Ready in about 30 minutes | Servings 3)
Per serving: 382 Calories; 22.1g Fat; 35.6g Carbs; 10.3g Protein; 3.1g Sugars

Ingredients

1 cup self-rising flour
1/2 teaspoon baking powder
1/2 teaspoon honey
1/2 stick butter, melted
1/2 cup Colby cheese, grated
1/2 cup buttermilk
1/4 teaspoon kosher salt
1 teaspoon dried parsley
1 teaspoon dried rosemary

Directions

Preheat your Air Fryer to 360 degrees F. Line the cooking basket with a piece of parchment paper. In a mixing bowl, thoroughly combine the flour, baking powder, honey, and butter. Gradually stir in the remaining ingredients.

Bake in the preheated Air Fryer for 15 minutes. Work in batches. Serve at room temperature. Bon appétit!

Favorite Spinach Cheese Pie

(Ready in about 30 minutes | Servings 4)
Per serving: 521 Calories; 33.9g Fat; 36.1g Carbs; 17.9g Protein; 5.2g Sugars

Ingredients

1 (16-ounce) refrigerated rolled pie crusts
4 eggs, beaten
1/2 cup buttermilk
1/2 teaspoon salt

1/2 teaspoon garlic powder

1/4 teaspoon cayenne pepper

2 cups spinach, torn into pieces

1 cup Swiss cheese, shredded

2 tablespoons scallions, chopped

Directions

Unroll the pie crust and press it into a cake pan, crimping the top edges if desired.

In a mixing dish, whisk together the eggs, buttermilk, salt, garlic, powder, and cayenne pepper.

Add the spinach, 1/2 of Swiss cheese, and scallions into the pie crust; pour the egg mixture over the top. Sprinkle the remaining 1/2 cup of Swiss cheese on top of the egg mixture.

Bake in the preheated Air Fryer at 350 degrees F for 10 minutes. Rotate the cake pan and bake an additional 10 minutes.

Transfer to a wire rack to cool for 5 to 10 minutes. Serve warm.

Greek-Style Pizza with Spinach and Feta

(Ready in about 20 minutes | Servings 2)

Per serving: 502 Calories; 29.5g Fat; 53.6g Carbs; 14.8g Protein; 17.3g Sugars

Ingredients

2 ounces frozen chopped spinach

Coarse sea salt, to taste

2 personal pizza crusts

1 tablespoon olive oil

1/4 cup tomato sauce

2 tablespoons fresh basil, roughly chopped

1/2 teaspoon dried oregano

1/2 feta cheese, crumbled

Directions

Add the frozen spinach to the saucepan and cook until all the liquid has evaporated, about 6 minutes. Season with sea salt to taste.

Preheat the Air Fryer to 395 degrees F.

Unroll the pizza dough on the Air Fryer baking tray; brush with olive oil.

Spread the tomato sauce over the pizza crust. Add the sautéed spinach, basil, and oregano. Sprinkle the feta cheese, covering the pizza crust to the edges.

Cook for 10 minutes, rotating your pizza halfway through the cooking time. Repeat with another pizza and serve warm.

Cheese and Bacon Crescent Ring

(Ready in about 25 minutes | Servings 4)

Per serving: 506 Calories; 30.8g Fat; 33.6g Carbs; 21.7g Protein; 6.9g Sugars

Ingredients

1 (8-ounce) can crescent dough sheet

1 ½ cups Monterey Jack cheese, shredded

4 slices bacon, cut chopped

4 tablespoons tomato sauce

1 teaspoon dried oregano

Directions

Unroll the crescent dough sheet and separate into 8 triangles. Arrange the triangles on a piece of parchment paper; place the triangles in the ring so it should look like the sun.

Place the shredded Monterey Jack cheese, bacon, and tomato sauce on the half of each triangle, at the center of the ring. Sprinkle with oregano.

Bring each triangle up over the filling. Press the overlapping dough to flatten. Transfer the parchment paper with the crescent ring to the Air Fryer basket.

Bake at 355 degrees F for 20 minutes or until the ring is golden brown. Bon appétit!

Crème Brûlée French Toast

(Ready in about 10 minutes | Servings 2)

Per serving: 407 Calories; 18.8g Fat; 51.7g Carbs; 8.3g Protein; 32.2g Sugars

Ingredients

4 slices bread, about 1-inch thick

2 tablespoons butter, softened

1 teaspoon ground cinnamon

2 ounces brown sugar

1/2 teaspoon vanilla paste

A pinch of sea salt

2 ounces Neufchâtel cheese, softened

Directions

In a mixing dish, combine the butter, cinnamon, brown sugar, vanilla, and salt. Spread the cinnamon butter on both sides of the bread slices. Arrange in the cooking basket. Cook at 390 degrees F for 2 minutes; turn over and cook an additional 2 minutes.

Serve with softened Neufchâtel cheese on individual plates. Bon appétit!

Puff Pastry Meat Strudel

(Ready in about 40 minutes | Servings 8)

Per serving: 356 Calories; 16g Fat; 35.6g Carbs; 16.5g Protein; 1.7g Sugars

Ingredients

1 tablespoon olive oil

1 small onion, chopped

2 garlic cloves, minced

1/3 pound ground beef

1/3 pound ground pork

2 tablespoons tomato puree

2 tablespoons matzo meal

Sea salt and ground black pepper, to taste

1/2 teaspoon cayenne pepper

1/4 teaspoon dried marjoram

2 cans (8-ounces) refrigerated crescent rolls

1 egg, whisked with 1 tablespoon of water

2 tablespoons sesame seeds

1/2 cup marinara sauce

1 cup sour cream

Directions

Heat the oil in a heavy skillet over medium flame. Sauté the onion just until soft and translucent. Add the garlic and sauté for 1 minute more.

Add the ground beef and pork and continue to cook for 3 minutes more or until the meat is no longer pink. Remove from the heat.

Add the tomato puree and matzo meal.

Roll out the puff pastry and spread the meat mixture lengthwise on the dough. Sprinkle with salt, black pepper, cayenne pepper, and marjoram. Fold in the sides of the dough over the meat mixture. Pinch the edges to seal.

Place the strudel on the parchment lined Air Fryer basket. Brush the strudel with the egg wash; sprinkle with sesame seeds.

Bake in the preheated Air Fryer at 330 degrees F for 18 to 20 minutes or until the pastry is puffed and golden and the filling is thoroughly cooked.

Allow your strudel to rest for 5 to 10 minutes before cutting and serving. Serve with the marinara sauce and sour cream on the side. Bon appétit!

Paella-Style Spanish Rice

(Ready in about 35 minutes | Servings 2)

Per serving: 546 Calories; 12.4g Fat; 90.7g Carbs; 17.6g Protein; 4.5g Sugars

Ingredients

2 cups water

1 cup white rice, rinsed and drained

1 cube vegetable stock

1 chorizo, sliced

2 cups brown mushrooms, cleaned and sliced

2 cloves garlic, finely chopped

1/2 teaspoon fresh ginger, ground

1 long red chili, minced

1/4 cup dry white wine

1/2 cup tomato sauce

1 teaspoon smoked paprika

Kosher salt and ground black pepper, to taste

1 cup green beans

Directions

In a medium saucepan, bring the water to a boil. Add the rice and vegetable stock cube. Stir and reduce the heat. Cover and let it simmer for 20 minutes.

Then, place the chorizo, mushrooms, garlic, ginger, and red chili in the baking pan. Cook at 380 degrees F for 6 minutes, stirring periodically. Add the prepared rice to the casserole dish. Add the remaining ingredients and gently stir to combine.

Cook for 6 minutes, checking periodically to ensure even cooking. Serve in individual bowls and enjoy!

Beef and Wild Rice Casserole

(Ready in about 50 minutes | Servings 3)
Per serving: 444 Calories; 13.1g Fat; 49.6g Carbs; 34.3g Protein; 4.7g Sugars

Ingredients

3 cups beef stock

1 cup wild rice, rinsed well

1 tablespoon olive oil

1/2 pound steak, cut into strips

1 carrot, chopped

1 medium-sized leek, chopped

2 garlic cloves, minced

1 chili pepper, minced

Kosher salt and ground black pepper, to your liking

Directions

Place beef stock and rice in a saucepan over medium-high heat.

Cover and bring it to a boil. Reduce the heat and let it simmer about 40 minutes. Drain the excess liquid and reserve.

Heat the olive oil in a heavy skillet over moderate heat. Cook the steak until no longer pink; place in the lightly greased baking pan.

Add carrot, leek, garlic, chili pepper, salt, and black pepper. Stir in the reserved wild rice. Stir to combine well.

Cook in the preheated Air Fryer at 360 degrees for 9 to 10 minutes. Serve immediately and enjoy!

Baked Tortilla Chips

(Ready in about 15 minutes | Servings 3)
Per serving: 167 Calories; 6.1g Fat; 26.4g Carbs; 3.2g Protein; 0.5g Sugars

Ingredients

1/2 (12-ounce) package corn tortillas

1 tablespoon canola oil

1/2 teaspoon chili powder

1 teaspoon salt

Directions

Cut the tortillas into small rounds using a cookie cutter.

Brush the rounds with canola oil. Sprinkle them with chili powder and salt.

Transfer to the lightly greased Air Fryer basket and bake at 360 degrees F for 5 minutes, shaking the basket halfway through. Bake until the chips are crisp, working in batches.

Serve with salsa or guacamole. Enjoy!

VEGAN

The Best Crispy Tofu

(Ready in about 55 minutes | Servings 4)

Per serving: 245 Calories; 13.3g Fat; 16.7g Carbs; 18.2g Protein; 1.2g Sugars

Ingredients

16 ounces firm tofu, pressed and cubed

1 tablespoon vegan oyster sauce

1 tablespoon tamari sauce

1 teaspoon cider vinegar

1 teaspoon pure maple syrup

1 teaspoon sriracha

1/2 teaspoon shallot powder

1/2 teaspoon porcini powder

1 teaspoon garlic powder

1 tablespoon sesame oil

5 tablespoons cornstarch

Directions

Toss the tofu with the oyster sauce, tamari sauce, vinegar, maple syrup, sriracha, shallot powder, porcini powder, garlic powder, and sesame oil. Let it marinate for 30 minutes.

Toss the marinated tofu with the cornstarch.

Cook at 360 degrees F for 10 minutes; turn them over and cook for 12 minutes more. Bon appétit!

Rainbow Roasted Vegetables

(Ready in about 25 minutes | Servings 4)

Per serving: 333 Calories; 23.4g Fat; 25.9g Carbs; 8.7g Protein; 8g Sugars

Ingredients

1 red bell pepper, seeded and cut into 1/2-inch chunks

1 cup squash, peeled and cut into 1/2-inch chunks

1 yellow bell pepper, seeded and cut into 1/2-inch chunks

1 yellow onion, quartered

1 green bell pepper, seeded and cut into 1/2-inch chunks

1 cup broccoli, broken into 1/2-inch florets

2 parsnips, trimmed and cut into 1/2-inch chunks

2 garlic cloves, minced

Pink Himalayan salt and ground black pepper, to taste

1/2 teaspoon marjoram

1/2 teaspoon dried oregano

1/4 cup dry white wine

1/4 cup vegetable broth

1/2 cup Kalamata olives, pitted and sliced

Directions

Arrange your vegetables in a single layer in the baking pan in the order of the rainbow (red, orange, yellow, and green). Scatter the minced garlic around the vegetables.

Season with salt, black pepper, marjoram, and oregano. Drizzle the white wine and vegetable broth over the vegetables.

Roast in the preheated Air Fryer at 390 degrees F for 15 minutes, rotating the pan once or twice. Scatter the Kalamata olives all over your vegetables and serve warm. Bon appétit!

Crispy Butternut Squash Fries

(Ready in about 25 minutes | Servings 4)
Per serving: 288 Calories; 7.6g Fat; 45.6g Carbs; 11.4g Protein; 3.1g Sugars

Ingredients

1 cup all-purpose flour
Salt and ground black pepper, to taste
3 tablespoons nutritional yeast flakes
1/2 cup almond milk
1/2 cup almond meal
1/2 cup bread crumbs
1 tablespoon herbs (oregano, basil, rosemary), chopped
1 pound butternut squash, peeled and cut into French fry shapes

Directions

In a shallow bowl, combine the flour, salt, and black pepper. In another shallow dish, mix the nutritional yeast flakes with the almond milk until well combined.

Mix the almond meal, breadcrumbs, and herbs in a third shallow dish. Dredge the butternut squash in the flour mixture, shaking off the excess. Then, dip in the milk mixture; lastly, dredge in the breadcrumb mixture.

Spritz the butternut squash fries with cooking oil on all sides.

Cook in the preheated Air Fryer at 400 degrees F approximately 12 minutes, turning them over halfway through the cooking time.

Serve with your favorite sauce for dipping. Bon appétit!

Easy Crispy Shawarma Chickpeas

(Ready in about 25 minutes | Servings 4)

Per serving: 150 Calories; 8.7g Fat; 14.2g Carbs; 4.4g Protein; 2.5g Sugars

Ingredients

1 (12-ounce) can chickpeas, drained and rinsed
2 tablespoons canola oil
1 teaspoon cayenne pepper
1 teaspoon sea salt
1 tablespoon Shawarma spice blend

Directions

Toss all ingredients in a mixing bowl.

Roast in the preheated Air Fryer at 380 degrees F for 10 minutes, shaking the basket halfway through the cooking time.

Work in batches. Bon appétit!

Caribbean-Style Fried Plantains

(Ready in about 20 minutes | Servings 2)
Per serving: 302 Calories; 14.2g Fat; 47.9g Carbs; 1.2g Protein; 21.6g Sugars

Ingredients

2 plantains, peeled and cut into slices
2 tablespoons avocado oil
2 teaspoons Caribbean Sorrel Rum Spice Mix

Directions

Toss the plantains with the avocado oil and spice mix.

Cook in the preheated Air Fryer at 400 degrees F for 10 minutes, shaking the cooking basket halfway through the cooking time.

Adjust the seasonings to taste and enjoy!

Famous Buffalo Cauliflower

(Ready in about 30 minutes | Servings 4)

Per serving: 306 Calories; 8.6g Fat; 50.3g Carbs; 9.7g Protein; 12.1g Sugars

Ingredients

1 pound cauliflower florets

1/2 cup all-purpose flour

1/2 cup rice flour

Sea salt and cracked black pepper, to taste

1/2 teaspoon cayenne pepper

1/2 teaspoon chili powder

1/2 cup soy milk

2 tablespoons soy sauce

2 tablespoons tahini

1 teaspoon vegetable oil

2 cloves garlic, minced

6 scotch bonnet peppers, seeded and sliced

1 small-sized onion, minced

1/2 teaspoon salt

1 cup water

2 tablespoons white vinegar

1 tablespoon granulated sugar

Directions

Rinse the cauliflower florets and pat them dry. Spritz the Air Fryer basket with cooking spray.

In a mixing bowl, combine the all purpose flour and rice flour; add the salt, black pepper, cayenne pepper, and chili powder.

Add the soy milk, soy sauce, and tahini. Stir until a thick batter is formed. Dip the cauliflower florets in the batter.

Cook the cauliflower at 400 degrees F for 16 minutes, turning them over halfway through the cooking time.

Meanwhile, heat the vegetable oil in a saucepan over medium-high heat; then, sauté the garlic, peppers, and onion for a minute or so or until they are fragrant.

Add the remaining ingredients and bring the mixture to a rapid boil. Now, reduce the heat to simmer, and continue cooking for 10 minutes more or until the sauce has reduced by half.

Pour the sauce over the prepared cauliflower and serve. Bon appétit!

Crunchy Eggplant Rounds

(Ready in about 45 minutes | Servings 4)

Per serving: 327 Calories; 8.5g Fat; 51.9g Carbs; 12.5g Protein; 7.3g Sugars

Ingredients

1 (1-pound) eggplant, sliced

1/2 cup flax meal

1/2 cup rice flour

Coarse sea salt and ground black pepper, to taste

1 teaspoon paprika

1 cup water

1 cup cornbread crumbs, crushed

1/2 cup vegan parmesan

Directions

Toss the eggplant with 1 tablespoon of salt and let it stand for 30 minutes. Drain and rinse well.

Mix the flax meal, rice flour, salt, black pepper, and paprika in a bowl. Then, pour in the water and whisk to combine well.

In another shallow bowl, mix the cornbread crumbs and vegan parmesan.

Dip the eggplant slices in the flour mixture, then in the crumb mixture; press to coat on all sides. Transfer to the lightly greased Air Fryer basket.

Cook at 370 degrees F for 6 minutes. Turn each slice over and cook an additional 5 minutes.

Serve garnished with spicy ketchup if desired. Bon appétit!

Classic Vegan Chili

(Ready in about 40 minutes | Servings 3)

Per serving: 335 Calories; 17.6g Fat; 37.3g Carbs; 11.5g Protein; 6.1g Sugars

Ingredients

1 tablespoon olive oil

1/2 yellow onion, chopped

2 garlic cloves, minced

2 red bell peppers, seeded and chopped

1 red chili pepper, seeded and minced

Sea salt and ground black pepper, to taste

1 teaspoon ground cumin

1 teaspoon cayenne pepper

1 teaspoon Mexican oregano

1/2 teaspoon mustard seeds

1/2 teaspoon celery seeds

1 can (28-ounces) diced tomatoes with juice

1 cup vegetable broth

1 (15-ounce) can black beans, rinsed and drained

1 bay leaf

1 teaspoon cider vinegar

1 avocado, sliced

Directions

Start by preheating your Air Fryer to 365 degrees F.

Heat the olive oil in a baking pan until sizzling. Then, sauté the onion, garlic, and peppers in the baking pan. Cook for 4 to 6 minutes.

Now, add the salt, black pepper, cumin, cayenne pepper, oregano, mustard seeds, celery seeds, tomatoes, and broth. Cook for 20 minutes, stirring every 4 minutes.

Stir in the canned beans, bay leaf, cider vinegar; let it cook for a further 8 minutes, stirring halfway through the cooking time.

Serve in individual bowls garnished with the avocado slices. Enjoy!

Dad's Roasted Pepper Salad

(Ready in about 25 minutes + chilling time | Servings 4)

Per serving: 296 Calories; 25.6g Fat; 15.6g Carbs; 4.6g Protein; 4.7g Sugars

Ingredients

2 yellow bell peppers

2 red bell peppers

2 green bell peppers

1 Serrano pepper

4 tablespoons olive oil

2 tablespoons cider vinegar

2 garlic cloves, peeled and pressed

1 teaspoon cayenne pepper

Sea salt, to taste

1/2 teaspoon mixed peppercorns, freshly crushed

1/2 cup pine nuts

1/4 cup loosely packed fresh Italian parsley leaves, roughly chopped

Directions

Start by preheating your Air Fryer to 400 degrees F. Brush the Air Fryer basket lightly with cooking oil.

Then, roast the peppers for 5 minutes. Give the peppers a half turn; place them back in the cooking basket and roast for another 5 minutes.

Turn them one more time and roast until the skin is charred and soft or 5 more minutes. Peel the peppers and let them cool to room temperature.

In a small mixing dish, whisk the olive oil, vinegar, garlic, cayenne pepper, salt, and crushed peppercorns. Dress the salad and set aside.

Add the pine nuts to the cooking basket. Roast at 360 degrees F for 4 minutes; give the nuts a good toss. Put the cooking basket back again and roast for a further 3 to 4 minutes.

Scatter the toasted nuts over the peppers and garnish with parsley. Bon appétit!

Cinnamon Pear Chips

(Ready in about 25 minutes | Servings 1)

Per serving: 133 Calories; 0.2g Fat; 35g Carbs; 0.6g Protein; 25.2g Sugars

Ingredients

1 medium pear, cored and thinly sliced

2 tablespoons cinnamon & sugar mixture

Directions

Toss the pear slices with the cinnamon & sugar mixture. Transfer them to the lightly greased Air Fryer basket.

Bake in the preheated Air Fryer at 380 degrees F for 8 minutes, turning them over halfway through the cooking time.

Transfer to wire rack to cool. Bon appétit!

Swiss Chard and Potato Fritters

(Ready in about 35 minutes | Servings 4)

Per serving: 492 Calories; 18.5g Fat; 66.7g Carbs; 16.9g Protein; 4.8g Sugars

Ingredients

8 baby potatoes

2 tablespoons olive oil

1 garlic clove, pressed

1/2 cup leeks, chopped

1 cup Swiss chard, torn into small pieces

Sea salt and ground black pepper, to your liking

1 tablespoon flax seed, soaked in 3 tablespoon water (vegan egg)

1 cup vegan cheese, shredded

1/4 cup chickpea flour

Directions

Start by preheating your Air Fryer to 400 degrees F.

Drizzle olive oil all over the potatoes. Place the potatoes in the Air Fryer basket and cook approximately 15 minutes, shaking the basket periodically.

Lightly crush the potatoes to split; mash the potatoes with the other ingredients.

Form the potato mixture into patties.

Bake in the preheated Air Fryer at 380 degrees F for 14 minutes, flipping them halfway through the cooking time. Bon appétit!

Veggie Fajitas with Simple Guacamole

(Ready in about 25 minutes | Servings 4)

Per serving: 307 Calories; 14.3g Fat; 40.2g Carbs; 8.2g Protein; 7.5g Sugars

Ingredients

1 tablespoon canola oil

1/2 cup scallions, thinly sliced

2 bell peppers, seeded and sliced into strips

1 habanero pepper, seeded and minced

1 garlic clove, minced

4 large Portobello mushrooms, thinly sliced

1/4 cup salsa

1 tablespoon yellow mustard

Kosher salt and ground black pepper, to taste

1/2 teaspoon Mexican oregano

1 medium ripe avocado, peeled, pitted and mashed

1 tablespoon fresh lemon juice

1/2 teaspoon onion powder

1/2 teaspoon garlic powder

1 teaspoon red pepper flakes

4 (8-inch) flour tortillas

Directions

Brush the sides and bottom of the cooking basket with canola oil. Add the scallions and cook for 1 to 2 minutes or until aromatic.

Then, add the peppers, garlic, and mushrooms to the cooking basket. Cook for 2 to 3 minutes or until tender.

Stir in the salsa, mustard, salt, black pepper, and oregano. Cook in the preheated Air Fryer at 380 degrees F for 15 minutes, stirring occasionally.

In the meantime, make your guacamole by mixing mashed avocado together with the lemon juice, garlic powder, onion powder, and red pepper flakes.

Divide between the tortillas and garnish with guacamole. Roll up your tortillas and enjoy!

Authentic Churros with Hot Chocolate

(Ready in about 25 minutes | Servings 3)

Per serving: 432 Calories; 15.8g Fat; 63.9g Carbs; 8.4g Protein; 24.7g Sugars

Ingredients

1/2 cup water

2 tablespoons granulated sugar

1/4 teaspoon sea salt

1 teaspoon lemon zest

1 tablespoon canola oil

1 cup all-purpose flour

2 ounces dark chocolate

1 cup milk

1 tablespoon cornstarch

1/3 cup sugar

1 teaspoon ground cinnamon

Directions

To make the churro dough, boil the water in a pan over medium-high heat; now, add the sugar, salt and lemon zest; cook until dissolved.

Add the canola oil and remove the pan from the heat. Gradually stir in the flour, whisking continuously until the mixture forms a ball.

Pour the mixture into a piping bag with a large star tip. Squeeze 4-inch strips of dough into the greased Air Fryer pan.

Cook at 410 degrees F for 6 minutes.

Meanwhile, prepare the hot chocolate for dipping. Melt the chocolate and 1/2 cup of milk in a pan over low heat.

Dissolve the cornstarch in the remaining 1/2 cup of milk; stir into the hot chocolate mixture. Cook on low heat approximately 5 minutes.

Mix the sugar and cinnamon; roll the churros in this mixture. Serve with the hot chocolate on the side. Enjoy!

Ooey-Gooey Dessert Quesadilla

(Ready in about 25 minutes | Servings 2)

Per serving: 476 Calories; 28.8g Fat; 45g Carbs; 9.2g Protein; 18.5g Sugars

Ingredients

1/4 cup blueberries

1/4 cup fresh orange juice

1/2 tablespoon maple syrup

1/2 cup vegan cream cheese

1 teaspoon vanilla extract

2 (6-inch) tortillas

2 teaspoons coconut oil

1/4 cup vegan dark chocolate

Directions

Bring the blueberries, orange juice, and maple syrup to a boil in a saucepan. Reduce the heat and let it simmer until the sauce thickens, about 10 minutes.

In a mixing dish, combine the cream cheese with the vanilla extract; spread on the tortillas. Add the blueberry filling on top. Fold in half.

Place the quesadillas in the greased Air Fryer basket. Cook at 390 degrees F for 10 minutes, until tortillas are golden brown and filling is melted. Make sure to turn them over halfway through the cooking.

Heat the coconut oil in a small pan and add the chocolate; whisk to combine well. Drizzle the chocolate sauce over the quesadilla and serve. Enjoy!

Couscous with Sun-Dried Tomatoes

(Ready in about 30 minutes | Servings 4)
Per serving: 230 Calories; 4.3g Fat; 41.3g Carbs; 7.2g Protein; 0.3g Sugars

Ingredients

1 cup couscous
1 cup boiled water
2 garlic cloves, pressed
1/3 cup coriander, chopped
1 cup shallots, chopped
4 ounces sun-dried tomato strips in oil
1 cup arugula lettuce, torn into pieces
2 tablespoons apple cider vinegar
Sea salt and ground black pepper, to taste

Directions

Put the couscous in a bowl; pour the boiling water, cover and set aside for 5 to 8 minutes; fluff with a fork.

Place the couscous in a lightly greased cake pan. Transfer the pan to the Air Fryer basket and cook at 360 digress F about 20 minutes. Make sure to stir every 5 minutes to ensure even cooking.

Transfer the prepared couscous to a nice salad bowl. Add the remaining ingredients; stir to combine and enjoy!

Thai Sweet Potato Balls

(Ready in about 50 minutes | Servings 4)

Per serving: 286 Calories; 6.1g Fat; 56.8g Carbs; 3.1g Protein; 33.7g Sugars

Ingredients

1 pound sweet potatoes
1 cup brown sugar
1 tablespoon orange juice
2 teaspoons orange zest
1/2 teaspoon ground cinnamon
1/4 teaspoon ground cloves
1/2 cup almond meal
1 teaspoon baking powder
1 cup coconut flakes

Directions

Bake the sweet potatoes at 380 degrees F for 30 to 35 minutes until tender; peel and mash them.

Add the brown sugar, orange juice, orange zest, ground cinnamon, cloves, almond meal, and baking powder; mix to combine well.

Roll the balls in the coconut flakes.

Bake in the preheated Air Fryer at 360 degrees F for 15 minutes or until thoroughly cooked and crispy.

Repeat the process until you run out of ingredients. Bon appétit!

Easy Granola with Raisins and Nuts

(Ready in about 40 minutes | Servings 8)
Per serving: 222 Calories; 14g Fat; 29.9g Carbs; 5.3g Protein; 11.3g Sugars

Ingredients

2 cups rolled oats
1/2 cup walnuts, chopped
1/3 cup almonds chopped
1/4 cup raisins
1/4 cup whole wheat pastry flour
1/2 teaspoon cinnamon

1/4 teaspoon nutmeg, preferably freshly grated

1/2 teaspoon salt

1/3 cup coconut oil, melted

1/3 cup agave nectar

1/2 teaspoon coconut extract

1/2 teaspoon vanilla extract

Directions

Thoroughly combine all ingredients. Then, spread the mixture onto the Air Fryer trays. Spritz with cooking spray.

Bake at 230 degrees F for 25 minutes; rotate the trays and bake 10 to 15 minutes more.

This granola can be stored in an airtight container for up to 2 weeks. Enjoy!

Indian Plantain Chips (Kerala Neenthram)

(Ready in about 30 minutes | Servings 2)

Per serving: 263 Calories; 9.4g Fat; 49.2g Carbs; 1.5g Protein; 21.3g Sugars

Ingredients

1 pound plantain, thinly sliced

1 tablespoon turmeric

2 tablespoons coconut oil

Directions

Fill a large enough cup with water and add the turmeric to the water.

Soak the plantain slices in the turmeric water for 15 minutes. Brush with coconut oil and transfer to the Air Fryer basket.

Cook in the preheated Air Fryer at 400 degrees F for 10 minutes, shaking the cooking basket halfway through the cooking time.

Serve at room temperature. Enjoy!

Aromatic Baked Potatoes with Chives

(Ready in about 45 minutes | Servings 2)

Per serving: 434 Calories; 14.1g Fat; 69g Carbs; 8.2g Protein; 5.1g Sugars

Ingredients

4 medium baking potatoes, peeled

2 tablespoons olive oil

1/4 teaspoon red pepper flakes

1/4 teaspoon smoked paprika

1 tablespoon sea salt

2 garlic cloves, minced

2 tablespoons chives, chopped

Directions

Toss the potatoes with the olive oil, seasoning, and garlic.

Place them in the Air Fryer basket. Cook in the preheated Air Fryer at 400 degrees F for 40 minutes or until fork tender.

Garnish with fresh chopped chives. Bon appétit!

Classic Baked Banana

(Ready in about 20 minutes | Servings 2)

Per serving: 202 Calories; 5.9g Fat; 40.2g Carbs; 1.1g Protein; 29g Sugars

Ingredients

2 just-ripe bananas

2 teaspoons lime juice

2 tablespoons honey

1/4 teaspoon grated nutmeg

1/2 teaspoon ground cinnamon

A pinch of salt

Directions

Toss the banana with all ingredients until well coated. Transfer your bananas to the parchment-lined cooking basket.

Bake in the preheated Air Fryer at 370 degrees F for 12 minutes, turning them over halfway through the cooking time. Enjoy!

Garlic-Roasted Brussels Sprouts with Mustard

(Ready in about 20 minutes | Servings 3)

Per serving: 151 Calories; 9.6g Fat; 14.5g Carbs; 5.4g Protein; 3.4g Sugars

Ingredients

1 pound Brussels sprouts, halved

2 tablespoons olive oil

Sea salt and freshly ground black pepper, to taste

2 garlic cloves, minced

1 tablespoon Dijon mustard

Directions

Toss the Brussels sprouts with the olive oil, salt, black pepper, and garlic.

Roast in the preheated Air Fryer at 380 degrees F for 15 minutes, shaking the basket occasionally. Serve with Dijon mustard and enjoy!

Italian-Style Risi e Bisi

(Ready in about 20 minutes | Servings 4)

Per serving: 434 Calories; 8.3g Fat; 79.8g Carbs; 9.9g Protein; 5g Sugars

Ingredients

2 cups brown rice

4 cups water

1/2 cup frozen green peas

3 tablespoons soy sauce

1 tablespoon olive oil

1 cup brown mushrooms, sliced

2 garlic cloves, minced

1 small-sized onion, chopped

1 tablespoon fresh parsley, chopped

Directions

Heat the brown rice and water in a pot over high heat. Bring it to a boil; turn the stove down to simmer and cook for 35 minutes. Allow your rice to cool completely.

Transfer the cold cooked rice to the lightly greased Air Fryer pan. Add the remaining ingredients and stir to combine.

Cook in the preheated Air Fryer at 360 degrees F for 18 to 22 minutes. Serve warm.

Tofu in Sweet & Sour Sauce

(Ready in about 25 minutes | Servings 3)

Per serving: 171 Calories; 7.1g Fat; 13.2g Carbs; 14.4g Protein; 6.2g Sugars

Ingredients

2 tablespoons Shoyu sauce

16 ounces extra-firm tofu, drained, pressed and cubed

1/2 cup water

1/4 cup pineapple juice

2 garlic cloves, minced

1/2 teaspoon fresh ginger, grated

1 teaspoon cayenne pepper

1/4 teaspoon ground black pepper

1/2 teaspoon salt

1 teaspoon honey

1 tablespoon arrowroot powder

Directions

Drizzle the Shoyu sauce all over the tofu cubes. Cook in the preheated Air Fryer at 380 degrees F for 6 minutes; shake the basket and cook for a further 5 minutes.

Meanwhile, cook the remaining ingredients in a heavy skillet over medium heat for 10 minutes, until the sauce has slightly thickened.

Stir the fried tofu into the sauce and continue cooking for 4 minutes more or until the tofu is thoroughly heated.

Serve warm and enjoy!

Gourmet Wasabi Popcorn

(Ready in about 30 minutes | Servings 2)
Per serving: 149 Calories; 11.7g Fat; 9.7g Carbs; 1.3g Protein; 0.6g Sugars

Ingredients

1/2 teaspoon brown sugar

1 teaspoon salt

1/2 teaspoon wasabi powder, sifted

1 tablespoon avocado oil

3 tablespoons popcorn kernels

Directions

Add the dried corn kernels to the Air Fryer basket; toss with the remaining ingredients.

Cook at 395 degrees F for 15 minutes, shaking the basket every 5 minutes. Work in two batches. Taste, adjust the seasonings and serve immediately. Bon appétit!

Baked Oatmeal with Berries

(Ready in about 30 minutes | Servings 4)
Per serving: 387 Calories; 24.1g Fat; 52.5g Carbs; 8.4g Protein; 25.9g Sugars

Ingredients

1 cup fresh strawberries

1/2 cup dried cranberries

1 ½ cups rolled oats

1/2 teaspoon baking powder

A pinch of sea salt

A pinch of grated nutmeg

1/2 teaspoon ground cinnamon

1/2 teaspoon vanilla extract

4 tablespoons agave syrup

1 ½ cups coconut milk

Directions

Spritz a baking pan with cooking spray.

Place 1/2 cup of strawberries on the bottom of the pan; place the cranberries over that.

In a mixing bowl, thoroughly combine the rolled oats, baking powder, salt, nutmeg, cinnamon, vanilla, agave syrup, and milk.

Pour the oatmeal mixtures over the fruits; allow it to soak for 15 minutes. Top with the remaining fruits.

Bake at 330 degrees F for 12 minutes. Serve warm or at room temperature. Enjoy!

Green Beans with Oyster Mushrooms

(Ready in about 20 minutes | Servings 3)
Per serving: 109 Calories; 6.4g Fat; 11.6g Carbs; 3.9g Protein; 2.9g Sugars

Ingredients

1 tablespoon extra-virgin olive oil

2 garlic cloves, minced

1/2 cup scallions, chopped

2 cups oyster mushrooms, sliced

12 ounces fresh green beans, trimmed

1 tablespoon soy sauce

Sea salt and ground black pepper, to taste

Directions

Start by preheating your Air Fryer to 390 degrees F. Heat the oil and sauté the garlic and scallions until tender and fragrant, about 5 minutes.

Add the remaining ingredients and stir to combine well.

Increase the temperature to 400 degrees F and cook for a further 5 minutes. Serve warm.

Hoisin-Glazed Bok Choy

(Ready in about 10 minutes | Servings 4)

Per serving: 235 Calories; 11.2g Fat; 6g Carbs; 25.7g Protein; 2.2g Sugars

Ingredients

1 pound baby Bok choy, bottoms removed, leaves separated

2 garlic cloves, minced

1 teaspoon onion powder

1/2 teaspoon sage

2 tablespoons hoisin sauce

2 tablespoons sesame oil

1 tablespoon all-purpose flour

Directions

Place the Bok choy, garlic, onion powder, and sage in the lightly greased Air Fryer basket.

Cook in the preheated Air Fryer at 350 degrees F for 3 minutes.

In a small mixing dish, whisk the hoisin sauce, sesame oil, and flour. Drizzle the sauce over the Bok choy. Cook for a further 3 minutes. Bon appétit!

Herb Roasted Potatoes and Peppers

(Ready in about 30 minutes | Servings 4)

Per serving: 158 Calories; 6.8g Fat; 22.6g Carbs; 1.8g Protein; 2.2g Sugars

Ingredients

1 pound russet potatoes, cut into 1-inch chunks

2 bell peppers, seeded and cut into 1-inch chunks

2 tablespoons olive oil

1 teaspoon dried rosemary

1 teaspoon dried basil

1 teaspoon dried oregano

1 teaspoon dried parsley flakes

Sea salt and ground black pepper, to taste

1/2 teaspoon smoked paprika

Directions

Toss all ingredients in the Air Fryer basket.

Roast at 400 degrees F for 15 minutes, tossing the basket occasionally. Work in batches.

Serve warm and enjoy!

DESSERTS

Dessert French Toast with Blackberries

(Ready in about 20 minutes | Servings 2)

Per serving: 324 Calories; 14.9g Fat; 42.2g Carbs; 6.5g Protein; 24.9g Sugars

Ingredients

2 tablespoons butter, at room temperature

1 egg

2 tablespoons granulated sugar

1/4 teaspoon ground cinnamon

1/4 teaspoon vanilla extract

6 slices French baguette

1 cup fresh blackberries

2 tablespoons powdered sugar

Direction

Start by preheating your Air Fryer to 375 degrees F.

In a mixing dish, whisk the butter, egg, granulated sugar, cinnamon and vanilla.

Dip all the slices of the French baguette in this mixture. Transfer the French toast to the baking pan.

Bake in the preheated Air Fryer for 8 minutes, turning them over halfway through the cooking time to ensure even cooking.

To serve, divide the French toast between two warm plates. Arrange the blackberries on top of each slice. Dust with powdered sugar and serve immediately. Enjoy!

Chocolate Lava Cake

(Ready in about 20 minutes | Servings 4)

Per serving: 450 Calories; 37.2g Fat; 24.2g Carbs; 5.6g Protein; 14.7g Sugars

Ingredients

4 ounces butter, melted

4 ounces dark chocolate

2 eggs, lightly whisked

4 tablespoons granulated sugar

2 tablespoons cake flour

1 teaspoon baking powder

1/2 teaspoon ground cinnamon

1/4 teaspoon ground star anise

Directions

Begin by preheating your Air Fryer to 370 degrees F. Spritz the sides and bottom of a baking pan with nonstick cooking spray.

Melt the butter and dark chocolate in a microwave-safe bowl. Mix the eggs and sugar until frothy.

Pour the butter/chocolate mixture into the egg mixture. Stir in the flour, baking powder, cinnamon, and star anise. Mix until everything is well incorporated.

Scrape the batter into the prepared pan. Bake in the preheated Air Fryer for 9 to 11 minutes.

Let stand for 2 minutes. Invert on a plate while warm and serve. Bon appétit!

Banana Chips with Chocolate Glaze

(Ready in about 20 minutes | Servings 2)

Per serving: 201 Calories; 7.5g Fat; 37.1g Carbs; 1.8g Protein; 22.9g Sugars

Ingredients

2 banana, cut into slices

1/4 teaspoon lemon zest

1 tablespoon agave syrup

1 tablespoon cocoa powder

1 tablespoon coconut oil, melted

Directions

Toss the bananas with the lemon zest and agave syrup. Transfer your bananas to the parchment-lined cooking basket.

Bake in the preheated Air Fryer at 370 degrees F for 12 minutes, turning them over halfway through the cooking time.

In the meantime, melt the coconut oil in your microwave; add the cocoa powder and whisk to combine well.

Serve the baked banana chips with a few drizzles of the chocolate glaze. Enjoy!

Grandma's Butter Cookies

(Ready in about 25 minutes | Servings 4)
Per serving: 492 Calories; 24.7g Fat; 61.1g Carbs; 6.7g Protein; 17.5g Sugars

Ingredients

8 ounces all-purpose flour

2 ½ ounces sugar

1 teaspoon baking powder

A pinch of grated nutmeg

A pinch of coarse salt

1 large egg, room temperature.

1 stick butter, room temperature

1 teaspoon vanilla extract

Directions

Mix the flour, sugar, baking powder, grated nutmeg, and salt in a bowl. In a separate bowl, whisk the egg, butter, and vanilla extract.

Stir the egg mixture into the flour mixture; mix to combine well or until it forms a nice, soft dough.

Roll your dough out and cut out with a cookie cutter of your choice.

Bake in the preheated Air Fryer at 350 degrees F for 10 minutes. Decrease the temperature to 330

degrees F and cook for 10 minutes longer. Bon appétit!

Cinnamon Dough Dippers

(Ready in about 20 minutes | Servings 6)
Per serving: 332 Calories; 14.8g Fat; 45.6g Carbs; 5.1g Protein; 27.6g Sugars

Ingredients

1/2 pound bread dough

1/4 cup butter, melted

1/2 cup caster sugar

1 tablespoon cinnamon

1/2 cup cream cheese, softened

1 cup powdered sugar

1/2 teaspoon vanilla

2 tablespoons milk

Directions

Roll the dough into a log; cut into 1-1/2 inch strips using a pizza cutter.

Mix the butter, sugar, and cinnamon in a small bowl. Use a rubber spatula to spread the butter mixture over the tops of the dough dippers.

Bake at 360 degrees F for 7 to 8 minutes, turning them over halfway through the cooking time. Work in batches.

Meanwhile, make the glaze dip by whisking the remaining ingredients with a hand mixer. Beat until a smooth consistency is reached.

Serve at room temperature and enjoy!

Chocolate Apple Chips

(Ready in about 15 minutes | Servings 2)

Per serving: 81 Calories; 0.5g Fat; 21.5g Carbs; 0.7g Protein; 15.9g Sugars

Ingredients

1 large Pink Lady apple, cored and sliced

1 tablespoon light brown sugar

A pinch of kosher salt

2 tablespoons lemon juice

2 teaspoons cocoa powder

Directions

Toss the apple slices with the other ingredients. Bake at 350 degrees F for 5 minutes; shake the basket to ensure even cooking and continue to cook an additional 5 minutes.

Bon appétit!

Favorite Apple Crisp

(Ready in about 40 minutes | Servings 4)

Per serving: 403 Calories; 18.6g Fat; 61.5g Carbs; 2.9g Protein; 40.2g Sugars

Ingredients

4 cups apples, peeled, cored and sliced

1/2 cup brown sugar

1 tablespoon honey

1 tablespoon cornmeal

1/4 teaspoon ground cloves

1/2 teaspoon ground cinnamon

1/4 cup water

1/2 cup quick-cooking oats

1/2 cup all-purpose flour

1/2 cup caster sugar

1/2 teaspoon baking powder

1/3 cup coconut oil, melted

Directions

Toss the sliced apples with the brown sugar, honey, cornmeal, cloves, and cinnamon. Divide

between four custard cups coated with cooking spray.

In a mixing dish, thoroughly combine the remaining ingredients. Sprinkle over the apple mixture.

Bake in the preheated Air Fryer at 330 degrees F for 35 minutes. Bon appétit!

Peppermint Chocolate Cheesecake

(Ready in about 40 minutes | Servings 6)

Per serving: 484 Calories; 36.7g Fat; 38.8g Carbs; 5g Protein; 22.2g Sugars

Ingredients

1 cup powdered sugar

1/2 cup all-purpose flour

1/2 cup butter

1 cup mascarpone cheese, at room temperature

4 ounces semisweet chocolate, melted

1 teaspoon vanilla extract

2 drops peppermint extract

Directions

Beat the sugar, flour, and butter in a mixing bowl. Press the mixture into the bottom of a lightly greased baking pan.

Bake at 350 degrees F for 18 minutes. Place it in your freezer for 20 minutes.

Then, make the cheesecake topping by mixing the remaining ingredients. Place this topping over the crust and allow it to cool in your freezer for a further 15 minutes. Serve well chilled.

Baked Coconut Doughnuts

(Ready in about 20 minutes | Servings 6)

Per serving: 305 Calories; 13.2g Fat; 40.1g Carbs; 6.7g Protein; 13.8g Sugars

Ingredients

1 ½ cups all-purpose flour

1 teaspoon baking powder

A pinch of kosher salt

A pinch of freshly grated nutmeg

1/2 cup white sugar

2 eggs

2 tablespoons full-fat coconut milk

2 tablespoons coconut oil, melted

1/4 teaspoon ground cardamom

1/4 teaspoon ground cinnamon

1 teaspoon coconut essence

1/2 teaspoon vanilla essence

1 cup coconut flakes

Directions

In a mixing bowl, thoroughly combine the all-purpose flour with the baking powder, salt, nutmeg, and sugar.

In a separate bowl, beat the eggs until frothy using a hand mixer; add the coconut milk and oil and beat again; lastly, stir in the spices and mix again until everything is well combined.

Then, stir the egg mixture into the flour mixture and continue mixing until a dough ball forms. Try not to over-mix your dough. Transfer to a lightly floured surface.

Roll out your dough to a 1/4-inch thickness using a rolling pin. Cut out the doughnuts using a 3-inch round cutter; now, use a 1-inch round cutter to remove the center.

Bake in the preheated Air Fryer at 340 degrees F approximately 5 minutes or until golden. Repeat with remaining doughnuts. Decorate with coconut flakes and serve.

Classic Vanilla Mini Cheesecakes

(Ready in about 40 minutes + chilling time | Servings 6)

Per serving: 321 Calories; 25g Fat; 17.1g Carbs; 8.1g Protein; 11.4g Sugars

Ingredients

1/2 cup almond flour

1 ½ tablespoons unsalted butter, melted

1 tablespoon white sugar

1 (8-ounce) package cream cheese, softened

1/4 cup powdered sugar

1/2 teaspoon vanilla paste

1 egg, at room temperature

Topping:

1 ½ cups sour cream

3 tablespoons white sugar

1 teaspoon vanilla extract

1/4 cup maraschino cherries

Directions

Thoroughly combine the almond flour, butter, and sugar in a mixing bowl. Press the mixture into the bottom of lightly greased custard cups.

Then, mix the cream cheese, 1/4 cup of powdered sugar, vanilla, and egg using an electric mixer on low speed. Pour the batter into the pan, covering the crust.

Bake in the preheated Air Fryer at 330 degrees F for 35 minutes until edges are puffed and the surface is firm.

Mix the sour cream, 3 tablespoons of white sugar, and vanilla for the topping; spread over the crust and allow it to cool to room temperature.

Transfer to your refrigerator for 6 to 8 hours. Decorate with maraschino cherries and serve well chilled.

Bakery-Style Hazelnut Cookies

(Ready in about 20 minutes | Servings 6)

Per serving: 450 Calories; 28.6g Fat; 43.9g Carbs; 8.1g Protein; 17.5g Sugars

Ingredients

1 ½ cups all-purpose flour

1 teaspoon baking soda

1 teaspoon fine sea salt

1 stick butter

1 cup brown sugar

2 teaspoons vanilla

2 eggs, at room temperature

1 cup hazelnuts, coarsely chopped

Directions

Begin by preheating your Air Fryer to 350 degrees F.

Mix the flour with the baking soda, and sea salt. In the bowl of an electric mixer, beat the butter, brown sugar, and vanilla until creamy. Fold in the eggs, one at a time, and mix until well combined. Slowly and gradually, stir in the flour mixture. Finally, fold in the coarsely chopped hazelnuts.

Divide the dough into small balls using a large cookie scoop; drop onto the prepared cookie sheets. Bake for 10 minutes or until golden brown, rotating the pan once or twice through the cooking time.

Work in batches and cool for a couple of minutes before removing to wire racks. Enjoy!

Chocolate Biscuit Sandwich Cookies

(Ready in about 20 minutes | Servings 10)

Per serving: 353 Calories; 18.6g Fat; 41.4g Carbs; 5.1g Protein; 16.1g Sugars

Ingredients

2 ½ cups self-rising flour

4 ounces brown sugar

1 ounce honey

5 ounces butter, softened

1 egg, beaten

1 teaspoon vanilla essence

4 ounces double cream

3 ounces dark chocolate

1 teaspoon cardamom seeds, finely crushed

Directions

Start by preheating your Air Fryer to 350 degrees F.

In a mixing bowl, thoroughly combine the flour, brown sugar, honey, and butter. Mix until your mixture resembles breadcrumbs.

Gradually, add the egg and vanilla essence. Shape your dough into small balls and place in the parchment-lined Air Fryer basket.

Bake in the preheated Air Fryer for 10 minutes. Rotate the pan and bake for another 5 minutes. Transfer the freshly baked cookies to a cooling rack.

As the biscuits are cooling, melt the double cream and dark chocolate in an air-fryer safe bowl at 350 degrees F. Add the cardamom seeds and stir well.

Spread the filling over the cooled biscuits and sandwich together. Bon appétit!

Easy Chocolate Brownies

(Ready in about 30 minutes | Servings 8)

Per serving: 200 Calories; 12.7g Fat; 21.7g Carbs; 2.5g Protein; 12.4g Sugars

Ingredients

1 stick butter, melted

1/2 cup caster sugar

1/2 cup white sugar

1 egg

1 teaspoon vanilla essence

1/2 cup all-purpose flour

1 teaspoon baking powder

1/2 cup cocoa powder

A pinch of salt

A pinch of ground cardamom

Directions

Start by preheating your Air Fryer to 350 degrees F. Now, spritz the sides and bottom of a baking pan with cooking spray.

In a mixing dish, beat the melted butter with sugar until fluffy. Next, fold in the egg and beat again.

After that, add the vanilla, flour, baking powder, cocoa, salt, and ground cardamom. Mix until everything is well combined.

Bake in the preheated Air Fryer for 20 to 22 minutes. Enjoy!

Light and Fluffy Chocolate Cake

(Ready in about 20 minutes | Servings 6)

Per serving: 242 Calories; 19.5g Fat; 13.6g Carbs; 4.7g Protein; 9.2g Sugars

Ingredients

1/2 stick butter, at room temperature

1/2 cup chocolate chips

2 tablespoons honey

2/3 cup almond flour

A pinch of fine sea salt

1 egg, whisked

1/2 teaspoon vanilla extract

Directions

Begin by preheating your Air Fryer to 330 degrees F.

In a microwave-safe bowl, melt the butter, chocolate, and honey.

Add the other ingredients to the cooled chocolate mixture; stir to combine well. Scrape the batter into a lightly greased baking pan.

Bake in the preheated Air Fryer for 15 minutes or until the center is springy and a toothpick comes out dry. Enjoy!

Cinnamon and Sugar Sweet Potato Fries

(Ready in about 30 minutes | Servings 2)

Per serving: 162 Calories; 2.1g Fat; 34.9g Carbs; 1.8g Protein; 18.1g Sugars

Ingredients

1 large sweet potato, peeled and sliced into sticks

1 teaspoon ghee

1 tablespoon cornstarch

1/4 teaspoon ground cardamom

1/4 cup sugar

1 tablespoon ground cinnamon

Directions

Toss the sweet potato sticks with the melted ghee and cornstarch.

Cook in the preheated Air Fryer at 380 degrees F for 20 minutes, shaking the basket halfway through the cooking time.

Sprinkle the cardamom, sugar, and cinnamon all over the sweet potato fries and serve. Bon appétit!

Easy Blueberry Muffins

(Ready in about 20 minutes | Servings 10)

Per serving: 191 Calories; 8g Fat; 25.7g Carbs; 4.3g Protein; 10.9g Sugars

Ingredients

1 ½ cups all-purpose flour

1/2 teaspoon baking soda

1 teaspoon baking powder

1/4 teaspoon kosher salt

1/2 cup granulated sugar

2 eggs, whisked

1/2 cup milk

1/4 cup coconut oil, melted

1/2 teaspoon vanilla paste

1 cup fresh blueberries

Directions

In a mixing bowl, combine the flour, baking soda, baking powder, sugar, and salt. Whisk to combine well.

In another mixing bowl, mix the eggs, milk, coconut oil, and vanilla.

Now, add the wet egg mixture to dry the flour mixture. Then, carefully fold in the fresh blueberries; gently stir to combine.

Scrape the batter mixture into the muffin cups. Bake your muffins at 350 degrees F for 12 minutes or until the tops are golden brown.

Sprinkle some extra icing sugar over the top of each muffin if desired. Serve and enjoy!

Chocolate Raspberry Wontons

(Ready in about 15 minutes | Servings 6)

Per serving: 356 Calories; 13g Fat; 51.2g Carbs; 7.9g Protein; 11.3g Sugars

Ingredients

1 (12-ounce) package wonton wrappers

6 ounces chocolate chips

1/2 cup raspberries, mashed

1 egg, lightly whisked + 1 tablespoon of water (egg wash)

1/4 cup caster sugar

Directions

Divide the chocolate chips and raspberries among the wonton wrappers. Now, fold the wrappers diagonally in half over the filling; press the edges with a fork.

Brush with the egg wash and seal the edges.

Bake at 370 degrees F for 8 minutes, flipping them halfway through the cooking time.

Work in batches. Sprinkle the caster sugar over your wontons and enjoy!

Country Pie with Walnuts

(Ready in about 20 minutes | Servings 6)

Per serving: 244 Calories; 19.1g Fat; 12.7g Carbs; 6.5g Protein; 10.9g Sugars

Ingredients

1 cup coconut milk

2 eggs

1/2 stick butter, at room temperature

1 teaspoon vanilla essence

1/4 teaspoon ground cardamom

1/4 teaspoon ground cloves

1/2 cup walnuts, ground

1/2 cup sugar

1/3 cup almond flour

Directions

Begin by preheating your Air Fryer to 360 degrees F. Spritz the sides and bottom of a baking pan with nonstick cooking spray.

Mix all ingredients until well combined. Scrape the batter into the prepared baking pan.

Bake approximately 13 minutes; use a toothpick to test for doneness. Bon appétit!

Cocktail Party Fruit Kabobs

(Ready in about 10 minutes | Servings 6)

Per serving: 165 Calories; 0.7g Fat; 41.8g Carbs; 1.6g Protein; 33.6g Sugars

Ingredients

2 pears, diced into bite-sized chunks

2 apples, diced into bite-sized chunks

2 mangos, diced into bite-sized chunks

1 tablespoon fresh lemon juice

1 teaspoon vanilla essence

2 tablespoons maple syrup

1 teaspoon ground cinnamon

1/2 teaspoon ground cloves

Directions

Toss all ingredients in a mixing dish.

Tread the fruit pieces on skewers.

Cook at 350 degrees F for 5 minutes. Bon appétit!

Sunday Banana Chocolate Cookies

(Ready in about 20 minutes | Servings 8)

Per serving: 298 Calories; 12.3g Fat; 45.9g Carbs; 3.8g Protein; 19.6g Sugars

Ingredients

1 stick butter, at room temperature

1 ¼ cups caster sugar

2 ripe bananas, mashed

1 teaspoon vanilla paste

1 2/3 cups all-purpose flour

1/3 cup cocoa powder

1 ½ teaspoons baking powder

1/4 teaspoon ground cinnamon

1/4 teaspoon crystallized ginger

1 ½ cups chocolate chips

Directions

In a mixing dish, beat the butter and sugar until creamy and uniform. Stir in the mashed bananas and vanilla.

In another mixing dish, thoroughly combine the flour, cocoa powder, baking powder, cinnamon, and crystallized ginger.

Add the flour mixture to the banana mixture; mix to combine well. Afterwards, fold in the chocolate chips.

Drop by large spoonfuls onto a parchment-lined Air Fryer basket. Bake at 365 degrees F for 11 minutes or until golden brown on the top. Bon appétit!

Rustic Baked Apples

(Ready in about 25 minutes | Servings 4)

Per serving: 211 Calories; 5.1g Fat; 45.5g Carbs; 2.6g Protein; 33.9g Sugars

Ingredients

4 Gala apples

1/4 cup rolled oats

1/4 cup sugar

2 tablespoons honey

1/3 cup walnuts, chopped

1 teaspoon cinnamon powder

1/2 teaspoon ground cardamom

1/2 teaspoon ground cloves

2/3 cup water

Directions

Use a paring knife to remove the stem and seeds from the apples, making deep holes.

In a mixing bowl, combine together the rolled oats, sugar, honey, walnuts, cinnamon, cardamom, and cloves.

Pour the water into an Air Fryer safe dish. Place the apples in the dish.

Bake at 340 degrees F for 17 minutes. Serve at room temperature. Bon appétit!

The Ultimate Berry Crumble

(Ready in about 40 minutes | Servings 6)

Per serving: 272 Calories; 8.3g Fat; 49.5g Carbs; 3.3g Protein; 31g Sugars

Ingredients

18 ounces cherries

1/2 cup granulated sugar

2 tablespoons cornmeal

1/4 teaspoon ground star anise

1/2 teaspoon ground cinnamon

2/3 cup all-purpose flour

1 cup demerara sugar

1/2 teaspoon baking powder

1/3 cup rolled oats

1/2 stick butter, cut into small pieces

Directions

Toss the cherries with the granulated sugar, cornmeal, star anise, and cinnamon. Divide between six custard cups coated with cooking spray.

In a mixing dish, thoroughly combine the remaining ingredients. Sprinkle over the berry mixture.

Bake in the preheated Air Fryer at 330 degrees F for 35 minutes. Bon appétit!

Mocha Chocolate Espresso Cake

(Ready in about 40 minutes | Servings 8)

Per serving: 320 Calories; 18.1g Fat; 35.9g Carbs; 4.1g Protein; 14.5g Sugars

Ingredients

1 ½ cups flour

2/3 cup sugar

1 teaspoon baking powder

1/4 teaspoon salt

1 stick butter, melted

1/2 cup hot strongly brewed coffee

1/2 teaspoon vanilla

1 egg

Topping:

1/4 cup flour

1/2 cup sugar

1/2 teaspoon ground cardamom

1 teaspoon ground cinnamon

3 tablespoons coconut oil

Directions

Mix all dry ingredients for your cake; then, mix in the wet ingredients. Mix until everything is well incorporated.

Spritz a baking pan with cooking spray. Scrape the batter into the baking pan.

Then make the topping by mixing all ingredients. Place on top of the cake. Smooth the top with a spatula.

Bake at 330 degrees F for 30 minutes or until the top of the cake springs back when gently pressed with your fingers. Serve with your favorite hot beverage. Bon appétit!

Chocolate and Peanut Butter Brownies

(Ready in about 30 minutes | Servings 10)

Per serving: 291 Calories; 7.9g Fat; 48.2g Carbs; 6.4g Protein; 32.3g Sugars

Ingredients

1 cup peanut butter

1 ¼ cups sugar

3 eggs

1 cup all-purpose flour

1 teaspoon baking powder

1/4 teaspoon kosher salt

1 cup dark chocolate, broken into chunks

Directions

Start by preheating your Air Fryer to 350 degrees F. Now, spritz the sides and bottom of a baking pan with cooking spray.

In a mixing dish, thoroughly combine the peanut butter with the sugar until creamy. Next, fold in the egg and beat until fluffy.

After that, stir in the flour, baking powder, salt, and chocolate. Mix until everything is well combined.

Bake in the preheated Air Fryer for 20 to 22 minutes. Transfer to a wire rack to cool before slicing and serving. Bon appétit!

Coconut Chip Cookies

(Ready in about 20 minutes | Servings 12)

Per serving: 304 Calories; 16.7g Fat; 34.2g Carbs; 4.3g Protein; 15.6g Sugars

Ingredients

1 cup butter, melted

1 ¾ cups granulated sugar

3 eggs

2 tablespoons coconut milk

1 teaspoon coconut extract

1 teaspoon vanilla extract

2 ¼ cups all-purpose flour

1/2 teaspoon baking powder

1/2 teaspoon baking soda

1/2 teaspoon fine table salt

2 cups coconut chips

Directions

Begin by preheating your Air Fryer to 350 degrees F.

In the bowl of an electric mixer, beat the butter and sugar until well combined. Now, add the eggs one at a time, and mix well; add the coconut milk, coconut extract, and vanilla; beat until creamy and uniform.

Mix the flour with baking powder, baking soda, and salt. Then, stir the flour mixture into the butter mixture and stir until everything is well incorporated.

Finally, fold in the coconut chips and mix again. Scoop out 1 tablespoon size balls of the batter on a cookie pan, leaving 2 inches between each cookie.

Bake for 10 minutes or until golden brown, rotating the pan once or twice through the cooking time.

Let your cookies cool on wire racks. Bon appétit!

Easy Chocolate and Coconut Cake

(Ready in about 20 minutes | Servings 10)

Per serving: 252 Calories; 18.9g Fat; 17.9g Carbs; 3.4g Protein; 13.8g Sugars

Ingredients

1 stick butter

1 ¼ cups dark chocolate, broken into chunks

1/4 cup tablespoon agave syrup

1/4 cup sugar

2 tablespoons milk

2 eggs, beaten

1/3 cup coconut, shredded

Directions

Begin by preheating your Air Fryer to 330 degrees F.

In a microwave-safe bowl, melt the butter, chocolate, and agave syrup. Allow it to cool to room temperature.

Add the remaining ingredients to the chocolate mixture; stir to combine well. Scrape the batter into a lightly greased baking pan.

Bake in the preheated Air Fryer for 15 minutes or until a toothpick comes out dry and clean. Enjoy!

OTHER AIR FRYER FAVORITES

Farmer's Breakfast Deviled Eggs

(Ready in about 25 minutes | Servings 3)

Per serving: 512 Calories; 42.9g Fat; 5.1g Carbs; 25.2g Protein; 3.6g Sugars

Ingredients

6 eggs

6 slices bacon

2 tablespoons mayonnaise

1 teaspoon hot sauce

1/2 teaspoon Worcestershire sauce

2 tablespoons green onions, chopped

1 tablespoon pickle relish

Salt and ground black pepper, to taste

1 teaspoon smoked paprika

Directions

Place the wire rack in the Air Fryer basket; lower the eggs onto the wire rack.

Cook at 270 degrees F for 15 minutes.

Transfer them to an ice-cold water bath to stop the cooking. Peel the eggs under cold running water; slice them into halves.

Cook the bacon at 400 degrees F for 3 minutes; flip the bacon over and cook an additional 3 minutes; chop the bacon and reserve.

Mash the egg yolks with the mayo, hot sauce, Worcestershire sauce, green onions, pickle relish, salt, and black pepper; add the reserved bacon and spoon the yolk mixture into the egg whites. Garnish with smoked paprika. Bon appétit!

Easy Greek Revithokeftedes

(Ready in about 30 minutes | Servings 3)

Per serving: 353 Calories; 4.1g Fat; 65.5g Carbs; 14.5g Protein; 6.3g Sugars

Ingredients

12 ounces canned chickpeas, drained

1 red onion, sliced

2 cloves garlic

1 chili pepper

1 tablespoon fresh coriander

2 tablespoons all-purpose flour

1/2 teaspoon cayenne pepper

Sea salt and freshly ground pepper, to taste

3 large (6 ½ -inch) pita bread

Directions

Pulse the chickpeas, onion, garlic, chili pepper and coriander in your food processor until the chickpeas are ground.

Add the all-purpose flour, cayenne pepper, salt, and black pepper; stir to combine well.

Form the chickpea mixture into balls and place them in the lightly greased Air Fryer basket.

Cook at 380 degrees F for about 15 minutes, shaking the basket occasionally to ensure even cooking.

Warm the pita bread in your Air Fryer at 390 degrees F for around 6 minutes.

Serve the revithokeftedes in pita bread with tzatziki or your favorite Greek topping. Enjoy!

Philadelphia Mushroom Omelet

(Ready in about 20 minutes | Servings 2)

Per serving: 272 Calories; 19.1g Fat; 8.1g Carbs; 18.3g Protein; 4.5g Sugars

Ingredients

1 tablespoon olive oil

1/2 cup scallions, chopped

1 bell pepper, seeded and thinly sliced

6 ounces button mushrooms, thinly sliced

4 eggs

2 tablespoons milk

Sea salt and freshly ground black pepper, to taste

1 tablespoon fresh chives, for serving

Directions

Heat the olive oil in a skillet over medium-high heat. Now, sauté the scallions and peppers until aromatic.

Add the mushrooms and continue to cook an additional 3 minutes or until tender. Reserve.

Generously grease a baking pan with nonstick cooking spray.

Then, whisk the eggs, milk, salt, and black pepper. Spoon into the prepared baking pan.

Cook in the preheated Air Fryer at 360 F for 4 minutes. Flip and cook for a further 3 minutes.

Place the reserved mushroom filling on one side of the omelet. Fold your omelet in half and slide onto a serving plate. Serve immediately garnished with fresh chives. Bon appétit!

Rosemary Roasted Mixed Nuts

(Ready in about 20 minutes | Servings 6)

Per serving: 295 Calories; 30.2g Fat; 5.8g Carbs; 4.8g Protein; 1.6g Sugars

Ingredients

2 tablespoons butter, at room temperature

1 tablespoon dried rosemary

1 teaspoon coarse sea salt

1/2 teaspoon paprika

1/2 cup pine nuts

1 cup pecans

1/2 cup hazelnuts

Directions

Toss all the ingredients in the mixing bowl.

Line the Air Fryer basket with baking parchment. Spread out the coated nuts in a single layer in the basket.

Roast at 350 degrees F for 6 to 8 minutes, shaking the basket once or twice. Work in batches. Enjoy!

Fingerling Potatoes with Cashew Sauce

(Ready in about 20 minutes | Servings 4)

Per serving: 341 Calories; 20.2g Fat; 34.2g Carbs; 9.8g Protein; 4.6g Sugars

Ingredients

1 pound fingerling potatoes

1 tablespoon butter, melted

Sea salt and ground black pepper, to your liking

1 teaspoon shallot powder

1 teaspoon garlic powder

Cashew Sauce:

1/2 cup raw cashews

1 teaspoon cayenne pepper

3 tablespoons nutritional yeast

2 teaspoons white vinegar

4 tablespoons water

1/4 teaspoon dried rosemary

1/4 teaspoon dried dill

Directions

Toss the potatoes with the butter, salt, black pepper, shallot powder, and garlic powder.

Place the fingerling potatoes in the lightly greased Air Fryer basket and cook at 400 degrees F for 6 minutes; shake the basket and cook for a further 6 minutes.

Meanwhile, make the sauce by mixing all ingredients in your food processor or high-speed blender.

Drizzle the cashew sauce over the potato wedges. Bake at 400 degrees F for 2 more minutes or until everything is heated through. Enjoy!

Brown Rice Bowl

(Ready in about 55 minutes | Servings 4)
Per serving: 302 Calories; 11g Fat; 41.2g Carbs; 9.4g Protein; 3.7g Sugars

Ingredients

1 cup brown rice
1 tablespoon peanut oil
2 tablespoons soy sauce
1/2 cup scallions, chopped
2 bell pepper, chopped
2 eggs, beaten
Sea salt and ground black pepper, to taste
1/2 teaspoon granulated garlic

Directions

Heat the brown rice and 2 ½ cups of water in a saucepan over high heat. Bring it to a boil; turn the stove down to simmer and cook for 35 minutes.

Grease a baking pan with nonstick cooking spray. Add the hot rice and the other ingredients.

Cook at 370 degrees F for 15 minutes, checking occasionally to ensure even cooking. Enjoy!

Fruit Skewers with a Greek Flair

(Ready in about 10 minutes | Servings 2)
Per serving: 194 Calories; 0.5g Fat; 49.2g Carbs; 3.1g Protein; 37.9g Sugars

Ingredients

6 strawberries, halved
1 banana, peeled and sliced
1/4 pineapple, peeled and cubed
1 teaspoon fresh lemon juice
1/4 cup Greek-Style yoghurt, optional
2 tablespoons honey
1 teaspoon vanilla

Directions

Toss the fruits with lemon juice in a mixing dish. Tread the fruit pieces on skewers.

Cook at 340 degrees F for 5 minutes.

Meanwhile, whisk the Greek yogurt with the honey and vanilla. Serve the fruit skewers with the Greek sauce on the side. Bon appétit!

Delicious Hot Fruit Bake

(Ready in about 40 minutes | Servings 4)
Per serving: 334 Calories; 7.4g Fat; 70g Carbs; 1.9g Protein; 60.9g Sugars

Ingredients

2 cups blueberries
2 cups raspberries
1 tablespoon cornstarch
3 tablespoons maple syrup
2 tablespoons coconut oil, melted
A pinch of freshly grated nutmeg
A pinch of salt
1 cinnamon stick
1 vanilla bean

Directions

Place your berries in a lightly greased baking dish. Sprinkle the cornstarch onto the fruit.

Whisk the maple syrup, coconut oil, nutmeg, and salt in a mixing dish; add this mixture to the berries and gently stir to combine.

Add the cinnamon and vanilla. Bake in the preheated Air Fryer at 370 degrees F for 35 minutes. Serve warm or at room temperature. Enjoy!

Jamaican Cornmeal Pudding

(Ready in about 1 hour + chilling time | Servings 6)
Per serving: 538 Calories; 21.5g Fat; 82.4g Carbs; 8.2g Protein; 49.4g Sugars

Ingredients

3 cups coconut milk
2 ounces butter, softened
1 teaspoon cinnamon
1/2 teaspoon grated nutmeg
1 cup sugar
1/2 teaspoon fine sea salt
1 ½ cups yellow cornmeal
1/4 cup all-purpose flour
1/2 cup water
1⁄2 cup raisins
1 teaspoon rum extract
1 teaspoon vanilla extract
Custard:
1/2 cup full-fat coconut milk
1 ounce butter
1/4 cup honey
1 dash vanilla

Directions

Place the coconut milk, butter, cinnamon, nutmeg, sugar, and salt in a large saucepan; bring to a rapid boil. Heat off.

In a mixing bowl, thoroughly combine the cornmeal, flour and water; mix to combine well.

Add the milk/butter mixture to the cornmeal mixture; mix to combine. Bring the cornmeal mixture to boil; then, reduce the heat and simmer approximately 7 minutes, whisking continuously. Remove from the heat. Now, add the raisins, rum extract, and vanilla.

Place the mixture into a lightly greased baking pan and bake at 325 degrees F for 12 minutes.

In a saucepan, whisk the coconut milk, butter, honey, and vanilla; let it simmer for 2 to 3 minutes. Now, prick your pudding with a fork and top with the prepared custard.

Return to your Air Fryer and bake for about 35 minutes more or until a toothpick inserted comes out dry and clean. Place in your refrigerator until ready to serve. Bon appétit!

Easy Frittata with Mozzarella and Kale

(Ready in about 20 minutes | Servings 3)
Per serving: 289 Calories; 19.6g Fat; 9.2g Carbs; 19.9g Protein; 5g Sugars

Ingredients

1 yellow onion, finely chopped
6 ounces wild mushrooms, sliced
6 eggs
1/4 cup double cream
1/2 teaspoon cayenne pepper
Sea salt and ground black pepper, to taste
1 tablespoon butter, melted
2 tablespoons fresh Italian parsley, chopped
2 cups kale, chopped
1/2 cup mozzarella, shredded

Directions

Begin by preheating the Air Fryer to 360 degrees F. Spritz the sides and bottom of a baking pan with cooking oil.

Add the onions and wild mushrooms, and cook in the preheated Air Fryer at 360 degrees F for 4 to 5 minutes.

In a mixing dish, whisk the eggs and double cream until pale. Add the spices, butter, parsley, and kale; stir until everything is well incorporated. Pour the mixture into the baking pan with the mushrooms.

Top with the cheese. Cook in the preheated Air Fryer for 10 minutes. Serve immediately and enjoy!

Mother's Day Pudding

(Ready in about 45 minutes | Servings 6)

Per serving: 548 Calories; 11.8g Fat; 92.2g Carbs; 14.9g Protein; 57.4g Sugars

Ingredients

1 pound French baguette bread, cubed

4 eggs, beaten

1/4 cup chocolate liqueur

1 cup granulated sugar

2 tablespoons honey

2 cups whole milk

1/2 cup heavy cream

1 teaspoon vanilla extract

1/4 teaspoon ground cloves

2 ounces milk chocolate chips

Directions

Place the bread cubes in a lightly greased baking dish. In a mixing bowl, thoroughly combine the eggs, chocolate liqueur, sugar, honey, milk, heavy cream, vanilla, and ground cloves.

Pour the custard over the bread cubes. Scatter the milk chocolate chips over the top of your bread pudding.

Let stand for 30 minutes, occasionally pressing with a wide spatula to submerge.

Cook in the preheated Air Fryer at 370 degrees F degrees for 7 minutes; check to ensure even cooking and cook an additional 5 to 6 minutes. Bon appétit!

Traditional Onion Bhaji

(Ready in about 40 minutes | Servings 3)

Per serving: 243 Calories; 13.8g Fat; 21.2g Carbs; 8.6g Protein; 3.6g Sugars

Ingredients

1 egg, beaten

2 tablespoons olive oil

2 onions, sliced

1 green chili, deseeded and finely chopped

2 ounces chickpea flour

1 ounce all-purpose flour

Salt and black pepper, to taste

1 teaspoon cumin seeds

1/2 teaspoon ground turmeric

Directions

Place all ingredients, except for the onions, in a mixing dish; mix to combine well, adding a little water to the mixture.

Once you've got a thick batter, add the onions; stir to coat well.

Cook in the preheated Air Fryer at 370 degrees F for 20 minutes flipping them halfway through the cooking time.

Work in batches and transfer to a serving platter. Enjoy!

Savory Italian Crespelle

(Ready in about 35 minutes | Servings 3)

Per serving: 451 Calories; 22.9g Fat; 36.1g Carbs; 25.1g Protein; 7.2g Sugars

Ingredients

3/4 cup all-purpose flour

2 eggs, beaten

1/4 teaspoon allspice

1/2 teaspoon salt

3/4 cup milk

1 cup ricotta cheese

1/2 cup Parmigiano-Reggiano cheese, preferably freshly grated

1 cup marinara sauce

Directions

Mix the flour, eggs, allspice, and salt in a large bowl. Gradually add the milk, whisking continuously, until well combined.

Let it stand for 20 minutes.

Spritz the Air Fryer baking pan with cooking spray. Pour the batter into the prepared pan.

Cook at 230 degrees F for 3 minutes. Flip and cook until browned in spots, 2 to 3 minutes longer.

Repeat with the remaining batter. Serve with the cheese and marinara sauce. Bon appétit!

Country-Style Apple Fries

(Ready in about 20 minutes | Servings 4)
Per serving: 219 Calories; 7.1g Fat; 34.3g Carbs; 5.1g Protein; 19.2g Sugars

Ingredients
1/2 cup milk

1 egg

1/2 all-purpose flour

1 teaspoon baking powder

4 tablespoons brown sugar

1 teaspoon vanilla extract

1/2 teaspoon ground cloves

A pinch of kosher salt

A pinch of grated nutmeg

1 tablespoon coconut oil, melted

2 Pink Lady apples, cored, peeled, slice into pieces (shape and size of French fries)

1/3 cup granulated sugar

1 teaspoon ground cinnamon

Directions
In a mixing bowl, whisk the milk and eggs; gradually stir in the flour; add the baking powder, brown sugar, vanilla, cloves, salt, nutmeg, and melted coconut oil. Mix to combine well.

Dip each apple slice into the batter, coating on all sides. Spritz the bottom of the cooking basket with cooking oil.

Cook the apple fries in the preheated Air Fryer at 395 degrees F approximately 8 minutes, turning them over halfway through the cooking time.

Cook in small batches to ensure even cooking.

In the meantime, mix the granulated sugar with the ground cinnamon; sprinkle the cinnamon sugar over the apple fries. Serve warm.

Grilled Cheese Sandwich

(Ready in about 15 minutes | Servings 1)
Per serving: 446 Calories; 31.9g Fat; 22.7g Carbs; 17.6g Protein; 3.7g Sugars

Ingredients
2 slices artisan bread

1 tablespoon butter, softened

1 tablespoon tomato ketchup

1/2 teaspoon dried oregano

2 slices Cheddar cheese

Directions
Brush one side of each slice of the bread with melted butter.

Add the tomato ketchup, oregano, and cheese. Make the sandwich and grill at 360 degrees F for 9 minutes or until cheese is melted. Bon appétit!

Green Pea Fritters with Parsley Yogurt Dip

(Ready in about 20 minutes | Servings 4)
Per serving: 233 Calories; 11.3g Fat; 23.8g Carbs; 9.4g Protein; 6.9g Sugars

Ingredients
Pea Fritters:

1 ½ cups frozen green peas

1 tablespoon sesame oil

1/2 cup scallions, chopped

2 garlic cloves, minced

1 cup chickpea flour

1 teaspoon baking powder

1/2 teaspoon sea salt

1/2 teaspoon ground black pepper

1/4 teaspoon dried dill

1/2 teaspoon dried basil

Parsley Yogurt Dip:

1/2 cup Greek-Style yoghurt

2 tablespoons mayonnaise

2 tablespoons fresh parsley, chopped

1 tablespoon fresh lemon juice

1/2 teaspoon garlic, smashed

Directions

Place the thawed green peas in a mixing dish; pour in hot water. Drain and rinse well.

Mash the green peas; add the remaining ingredients for the pea fritters and mix to combine well. Shape the mixture into patties and transfer them to the lightly greased cooking basket.

Bake at 330 degrees F for 14 minutes or until thoroughly heated.

Meanwhile, make your dipping sauce by whisking the remaining ingredients. Place in your refrigerator until ready to serve.

Serve the green pea fritters with the chilled dip on the side. Enjoy!

Baked Eggs Florentine

(Ready in about 20 minutes | Servings 2)

Per serving: 325 Calories; 25.1g Fat; 5.1g Carbs; 19.1g Protein; 2.2g Sugars

Ingredients

1 tablespoon ghee, melted

2 cups baby spinach, torn into small pieces

2 tablespoons shallots, chopped

1/4 teaspoon red pepper flakes

Salt, to taste

1 tablespoon fresh thyme leaves, roughly chopped

4 eggs

Directions

Start by preheating your Air Fryer to 350 degrees F. Brush the sides and bottom of a gratin dish with the melted ghee.

Put the spinach and shallots into the bottom of the gratin dish. Season with red pepper, salt, and fresh thyme.

Make four indents for the eggs; crack one egg into each indent. Bake for 12 minutes, rotating the pan once or twice to ensure even cooking. Enjoy!

Bagel 'n' Egg Melts

(Ready in about 25 minutes | Servings 3)

Per serving: 575 Calories; 29.4g Fat; 50.8g Carbs; 26.6g Protein; 7.5g Sugars

Ingredients

3 eggs

3 slices smoked ham, chopped

1 teaspoon Dijon mustard

1/4 cup mayonnaise

Salt and white pepper, to taste

3 bagels

3 ounces Colby cheese, shredded

Directions

Place the wire rack in the Air Fryer basket; lower the eggs onto the wire rack.

Cook at 270 degrees F for 15 minutes.

Transfer them to an ice-cold water bath to stop the cooking. Peel the eggs under cold running water; coarsely chop them and set aside.

Combine the chopped eggs, ham, mustard, mayonnaise, salt, and pepper in a mixing bowl.

Slice the bagels in half. Spread the egg mixture on top and sprinkle with the shredded cheese.

Grill in the preheated Air Fryer at 360 degrees F for 7 minutes or until cheese is melted. Bon appétit!

Italian Sausage and Veggie Bake

(Ready in about 20 minutes | Servings 4)
Per serving: 537 Calories; 35.6g Fat; 16.3g Carbs; 37.2g Protein; 5.9g Sugars

Ingredients

1 pound Italian sausage

2 red peppers, seeded and sliced

2 green peppers, seeded and sliced

1 cup mushrooms, sliced

1 shallot, sliced

4 cloves garlic

1 teaspoon dried basil

1 teaspoon dried oregano

1/4 teaspoon black pepper

1/4 teaspoon cayenne pepper

Sea salt, to taste

2 tablespoons Dijon mustard

1 cup chicken broth

Directions

Toss all ingredients in a lightly greased baking pan. Make sure the sausages and vegetables are coated with the oil and seasonings.

Bake in the preheated Air Fryer at 380 degrees F for 15 minutes.

Divide between individual bowls and serve warm. Bon appétit!

Greek-Style Roasted Figs

(Ready in about 20 minutes | Servings 4)
Per serving: 209 Calories; 4.2g Fat; 43.6g Carbs; 2.9g Protein; 40.3g Sugars

Ingredients

2 teaspoons butter, melted

8 figs, halved

2 tablespoons brown sugar

1/2 teaspoon cinnamon

1 teaspoon lemon zest

1 cup Greek yogurt

4 tablespoons honey

Directions

Drizzle the melted butter all over the fig halves. Sprinkle brown sugar, cinnamon, and lemon zest on the fig slices. Meanwhile, mix the Greek yogurt with the honey.

Roast in the preheated Air Fryer at 330 degrees F for 16 minutes.

To serve, divide the figs among 4 bowls and serve with a dollop of the yogurt sauce. Enjoy!

Classic Egg Salad

(Ready in about 20 minutes + chilling time | Servings 3)
Per serving: 294 Calories; 21.2g Fat; 10.5g Carbs; 14.9g Protein; 4.9g Sugars

Ingredients

6 eggs

1 teaspoon mustard

1/2 cup mayonnaise

1 tablespoons white vinegar

2 carrots, trimmed and sliced

1 red bell pepper, seeded and sliced

1 green bell pepper, seeded and sliced

1 shallot, sliced

Sea salt and ground black pepper, to taste

Directions

Place the wire rack in the Air Fryer basket; lower the eggs onto the wire rack.

Cook at 270 degrees F for 15 minutes.

Transfer them to an ice-cold water bath to stop the cooking. Peel the eggs under cold running water; coarsely chop the hard-boiled eggs and set aside.

Toss with the remaining ingredients and serve well chilled. Bon appétit!

Breakfast Muffins with Mushrooms and Goat Cheese

(Ready in about 25 minutes | Servings 6)

Per serving: 278 Calories; 21.5g Fat; 5.5g Carbs; 15.2g Protein; 3.3g Sugars

Ingredients

2 tablespoons butter, melted

1 yellow onion, chopped

2 garlic cloves, minced

1 cup brown mushrooms, sliced

Sea salt and ground black pepper, to taste

1 teaspoon fresh basil

8 eggs, lightly whisked

6 tablespoons goat cheese, crumbled

Directions

Start by preheating your Air Fryer to 330 degrees F. Now, spritz a 6-tin muffin tin with cooking spray.

Melt the butter in a heavy-bottomed skillet over medium-high heat. Sauté the onions, garlic, and mushrooms until just tender and fragrant.

Add the salt, black pepper, and basil and remove from heat. Divide out the sautéed mixture into the muffin tin.

Pour the whisked eggs on top and top with the goat cheese. Bake for 20 minutes rotating the pan halfway through the cooking time. Bon appétit!

Scrambled Eggs with Sausage

(Ready in about 25 minutes | Servings 6)

Per serving: 204 Calories; 11.5g Fat; 8.7g Carbs; 15.6g Protein; 1.1g Sugars

Ingredients

1 teaspoon lard

1/2 pound turkey sausage

6 eggs

1 scallion, chopped

1 garlic clove, minced

1 sweet pepper, seeded and chopped

1 chili pepper, seeded and chopped

Sea salt and ground black pepper, to taste

1/2 cup Swiss cheese, shredded

Directions

Start by preheating your Air Fryer to 330 degrees F. Now, spritz 6 silicone molds with cooking spray.

Melt the lard in a saucepan over medium-high heat. Now, cook the sausage for 5 minutes or until no longer pink.

Coarsely chop the sausage; add the eggs, scallions, garlic, peppers, salt, and black pepper. Divide the egg mixture between the silicone molds. Top with the shredded cheese.

Bake in the preheated Air Fryer at 340 degrees F for 15 minutes, checking halfway through the cooking time to ensure even cooking. Enjoy!

Southwest Bean Potpie

(Ready in about 30 minutes | Servings 5)

Per serving: 459 Calories; 26.3g Fat; 47.9g Carbs; 10.4g Protein; 12.5g Sugars

Ingredients

1 tablespoon olive oil

2 sweet peppers, seeded and sliced

1 carrot, chopped

1 onion, chopped

2 garlic cloves, minced

1 cup cooked bacon, diced

1 ½ cups beef bone broth

20 ounces canned red kidney beans, drained

Sea salt and freshly ground black pepper, to taste

1 package (8 1/2-ounce) cornbread mix

1/2 cup milk

2 tablespoons butter, melted

Directions

Heat the olive oil in a saucepan over medium-high heat. Now, cook the peppers, carrot, onion, and garlic until they have softened, about 7 minutes

Add the bacon and broth. Bring to a boil and cook for 2 minutes more. Stir in the kidney beans, salt and black pepper; continue to cook until everything is heated through.

Transfer the mixture to the lightly greased baking pan.

In a small bowl, combine the muffin mix, milk, and melted butter. Stir until well mixed and spoon evenly over the bean mixture. Smooth it with a spatula and transfer to the Air Fryer cooking basket.

Bake in the preheated Air Fryer at 400 degrees F for 12 minutes. Place on a wire rack to cool slightly before slicing and serving. Bon appétit!

Veggie Casserole with Ham and Baked Eggs

(Ready in about 30 minutes | Servings 4)
Per serving: 325 Calories; 20.9g Fat; 7.9g Carbs; 26.6g Protein; 2.8g Sugars

Ingredients

2 tablespoons butter, melted
1 zucchini, diced
1 bell pepper, seeded and sliced
1 red chili pepper, seeded and minced
1 medium-sized leek, sliced
3/4 pound ham, cooked and diced
5 eggs
1 teaspoon cayenne pepper
Sea salt, to taste
1/2 teaspoon ground black pepper
1 tablespoon fresh cilantro, chopped

Directions

Start by preheating the Air Fryer to 380 degrees F. Grease the sides and bottom of a baking pan with the melted butter.

Place the zucchini, peppers, leeks and ham in the baking pan. Bake in the preheated Air Fryer for 6 minutes.

Crack the eggs on top of ham and vegetables; season with the cayenne pepper, salt, and black pepper. Bake for a further 20 minutes or until the whites are completely set.

Garnish with fresh cilantro and serve. Bon appétit!

French Toast with Blueberries and Honey

(Ready in about 20 minutes | Servings 6)
Per serving: 275 Calories; 14.4g Fat; 27.8g Carbs; 8.5g Protein; 10.9g Sugars

Ingredients

1/4 cup milk
2 eggs
2 tablespoons butter, melted
1/2 teaspoon ground cinnamon
1/4 teaspoon ground cloves
1 teaspoon vanilla extract
6 slices day-old French baguette
2 tablespoons honey
1/2 cup blueberries

Directions

In a mixing bowl, whisk the milk eggs, butter, cinnamon, cloves, and vanilla extract.

Dip each piece of the baguette into the egg mixture and place in the parchment-lined Air Fryer basket.

Cook in the preheated Air Fryer at 360 degrees F for 6 to 7 minutes, turning them over halfway through the cooking time to ensure even cooking. Serve garnished with honey and blueberries. Enjoy!

Carrot Fries with Romano Cheese

(Ready in about 20 minutes | Servings 3)

Per serving: 122 Calories; 10g Fat; 4.2g Carbs; 4.1g Protein; 0.4g Sugars

Ingredients

3 carrots, sliced into sticks

1 tablespoon coconut oil

1/3 cup Romano cheese, preferably freshly grated

2 teaspoons granulated garlic

Sea salt and ground black pepper, to taste

Directions

Toss all ingredients in a mixing bowl until the carrots are coated on all sides.

Cook at 380 degrees F for 15 minutes, shaking the basket halfway through the cooking time.

Serve with your favorite dipping sauce. Bon appétit!

Quinoa with Baked Eggs and Bacon

(Ready in about 40 minutes | Servings 4)

Per serving: 416 Calories; 25.8g Fat; 27.9g Carbs; 17.8g Protein; 2.7g Sugars

Ingredients

1/2 cup quinoa

1/2 pound potatoes, diced

1 onion, diced

6 slices bacon, precooked

1 tablespoon butter, melted

Sea salt and ground black pepper, to taste

6 eggs

Directions

Rinse the quinoa under cold running water. Place the rinsed quinoa in a pan and add 1 cup of water.

Bring it to the boil. Turn the heat down and let it simmer for 13 to 15 minutes or until tender; reserve.

Place the diced potatoes and onion in a lightly greased casserole dish. Add the bacon and the reserved quinoa. Drizzle the melted butter over the quinoa and sprinkle with salt and pepper.

Bake in the preheated Air Fryer at 390 degrees F for 10 minutes.

Turn the temperature down to 350 degrees F.

Make six indents for the eggs; crack one egg into each indent. Bake for 12 minutes, rotating the pan once or twice to ensure even cooking. Enjoy!

Famous Western Eggs

(Ready in about 20 minutes | Servings 6)

Per serving: 336 Calories; 22.6g Fat; 7.2g Carbs; 25.1g Protein; 4.7g Sugars

Ingredients

6 eggs

3/4 cup milk

1 ounce cream cheese, softened

Sea salt, to your liking

1/4 teaspoon ground black pepper

1/4 teaspoon paprika

6 ounces cooked ham, diced

1 onion, chopped

1/3 cup cheddar cheese, shredded

Directions

Begin by preheating the Air Fryer to 360 degrees F. Spritz the sides and bottom of a baking pan with cooking oil.

In a mixing dish, whisk the eggs, milk, and cream cheese until pale. Add the spices, ham, and onion; stir until everything is well incorporated.

Pour the mixture into the baking pan; top with the cheddar cheese.

Bake in the preheated Air Fryer for 12 minutes. Serve warm and enjoy!

Celery Fries with Harissa Mayo

(Ready in about 30 minutes | Servings 3)

Per serving: 233 Calories; 23.7g Fat; 4.3g Carbs; 1.3g Protein; 1.9g Sugars

Ingredients

1/2 pound celery root
2 tablespoons olive oil
Sea salt and ground black pepper, to taste
Harissa Mayo
1/4 cup mayonnaise
2 tablespoons sour cream
1/2 tablespoon harissa paste
1/4 teaspoon ground cumin
Salt, to taste

Directions

Cut the celery root into desired size and shape. Then, preheat your Air Fryer to 400 degrees F. Now, spritz the Air Fryer basket with cooking spray.

Toss the celery fries with the olive oil, salt, and black pepper. Bake in the preheated Air Fryer for 25 to 30 minutes, turning them over every 10 minutes to promote even cooking.

Meanwhile, mix all ingredients for the harissa mayo. Place in your refrigerator until ready to serve. Bon appétit!

English Muffins with a Twist

(Ready in about 15 minutes | Servings 4)

Per serving: 289 Calories; 9.3g Fat; 42.2g Carbs; 10.2g Protein; 17.3g Sugars

Ingredients

4 English muffins, split in half
2 eggs
1/3 cup milk
1/4 cup heavy cream
2 tablespoons honey
1 teaspoon pure vanilla extract
1/4 cup confectioners' sugar

Directions

Cut the muffins crosswise into strips.

In a mixing bowl, whisk the eggs, milk, heavy cream, honey, and vanilla extract.

Dip each piece of muffins into the egg mixture and place in the parchment-lined Air Fryer basket.

Cook in the preheated Air Fryer at 360 degrees F for 6 to 7 minutes, turning them over halfway through the cooking time to ensure even cooking. Dust with confectioners' sugar and serve warm.

Easy Roasted Hot Dogs

(Ready in about 25 minutes | Servings 6)

Per serving: 415 Calories; 15.2g Fat; 41.4g Carbs; 28.1g Protein; 11.8g Sugars

Ingredients

6 hot dogs
6 hot dog buns
1 tablespoon mustard
6 tablespoons ketchup
6 lettuce leaves

Directions

Place the hot dogs in the lightly greased Air Fryer basket.

Bake at 380 degrees F for 15 minutes, turning them over halfway through the cooking time to promote even cooking.

Place on the bun and add the mustard, ketchup, and lettuce leaves. Enjoy!

Rum Roasted Cherries

(Ready in about 40 minutes | Servings 3)

Per serving: 128 Calories; 0.2g Fat; 24.7g Carbs; 0.9g Protein; 21.8g Sugars

Ingredients

9 ounces dark sweet cherries

2 tablespoons brown sugar

1 tablespoon honey

3 tablespoons rum

A pinch of grated nutmeg

1/4 teaspoon ground cloves

1/4 teaspoon ground cardamom

1 teaspoon vanilla

Directions

Place the cherries in a lightly greased baking dish. Whisk the remaining ingredients until everything is well combined; add this mixture to the baking dish and gently stir to combine.

Bake in the preheated Air Fryer at 370 degrees F for 35 minutes. Serve at room temperature. Bon appétit!

Mediterranean Roasted Vegetable and Bean Salad

(Ready in about 20 minutes | Servings 4)

Per serving: 209 Calories; 17.6g Fat; 11.3g Carbs; 4.1g Protein; 4.8g Sugars

Ingredients

1 red onion, sliced

1 pound cherry tomatoes

1/2 pound asparagus

1 cucumber, sliced

2 cups baby spinach

2 tablespoons white vinegar

1/4 cup extra-virgin olive oil

2 tablespoons fresh parsley

Sea salt and pepper to taste

8 ounces canned red kidney beans, rinsed

1/2 cup Kalamata olives, pitted and sliced

Directions

Begin by preheating your Air Fryer to 400 degrees F.

Place the onion, cherry tomatoes, and asparagus in the lightly greased Air Fryer basket. Bake for 5 to 6 minutes, tossing the basket occasionally.

Transfer to a salad bowl. Add the cucumber and baby spinach.

Then, whisk the vinegar, olive oil, parsley, salt, and black pepper in a small mixing bowl. Dress your salad; add the beans and olives.

Toss to combine well and serve.

Easiest Vegan Burrito Ever

(Ready in about 35 minutes | Servings 6)

Per serving: 344 Calories; 8g Fat; 57.1g Carbs; 15.2g Protein; 4.4g Sugars

Ingredients

2 tablespoons olive oil

1 small onion, chopped

2 sweet peppers, seeded and chopped

1 chili pepper, seeded and minced

Sea salt and ground black pepper, to taste

1 teaspoon red pepper flakes, crushed

1 teaspoon dried parsley flakes

10 ounces cooked pinto beans

12 ounces canned sweet corn, drained

6 large corn tortillas

1/2 cup vegan sour cream

Directions

Begin by preheating your Air Frye to 400 degrees F.

Heat the olive oil in a baking pan. Once hot, cook the onion and peppers until they are tender and fragrant, about 15 minutes.

Stir in the salt, black pepper, red pepper, parsley, beans, and sweet corn; stir to combine well.

Divide the bean mixture between the corn tortillas. Roll up your tortillas and place them on the parchment-lined Air Fryer basket.

Bake in the preheated Air Fryer at 350 degrees F for 15 minutes. Serve garnished with sour cream. Bon appétit!

Bourbon Glazed Mango with Walnuts

(Ready in about 20 minutes | Servings 4)

Per serving: 251 Calories; 13.9g Fat; 32.5g Carbs; 2.9g Protein; 29g Sugars

Ingredients

2 ripe mangos, peeled and diced

2 tablespoons bourbon whiskey

2 tablespoons sugar

2 tablespoons coconut oil, melted

1/4 teaspoon ground cardamom

1 teaspoon vanilla essence

1/4 teaspoon pure coconut extract

1/2 cup walnuts, coarsely chopped

Directions

Start by preheating your Air Fryer to 400 degrees F.

Toss all ingredients in a baking dish and transfer to the Air fryer basket.

Now, bake for 10 minutes, or until browned on top. Serve with whipped cream if desired. Bon appétit!

Baked Apples with Crisp Topping

(Ready in about 25 minutes | Servings 3)

Per serving: 294 Calories; 9.5g Fat; 57.3g Carbs; 4.6g Protein; 35.8g Sugars

Ingredients

3 Granny Smith apples, cored

2/3 cup rolled oats

3 tablespoons honey

1 tablespoon fresh orange juice

1/2 teaspoon ground cardamom

1/2 teaspoon ground cinnamon

1/4 teaspoon ground cloves

1/4 teaspoon ground star anise

2 tablespoons butter, cut in pieces

3 tablespoons cranberries

Directions

Use a paring knife to remove the stem and seeds from the apples, making deep holes.

In a mixing bowl, combine together the rolled oats, honey, orange juice, cardamom, cinnamon, cloves, anise, butter, and cranberries.

Pour enough water into an Air Fryer safe dish. Place the apples in the dish.

Bake at 340 degrees F for 16 to 18 minutes. Serve at room temperature. Bon appétit!

Crunch-Crunch Party Mix

(Ready in about 25 minutes | Servings 8)

Per serving: 409 Calories; 27.1g Fat; 28.2g Carbs; 17.1g Protein; 1.8g Sugars

Ingredients

1 cup whole-grain Rice Chex

2 cups cheese squares

1 cup pistachios

1/2 cup almonds

1 cup cheddar-flavored mini pretzel twists

2 tablespoons butter, melted

1/4 cup poppy seeds

1/2 cup sunflower seeds

1 tablespoon coarse sea salt

1 tablespoon garlic powder

1 tablespoon paprika

Directions

Mix all ingredients in a large bowl. Toss to combine well.

Place in a single layer in the parchment-lined cooking basket.

Bake in the preheated Air Fryer at 310 degrees F for 13 to 16 minutes. Allow it to cool completely before serving.

Store in an airtight container for up to 3 months. Bon appétit!

Homemade Pork Scratchings

(Ready in about 50 minutes | Servings 10)

Per serving: 245 Calories; 14.1g Fat; 0g Carbs; 27.6g Protein; 0g Sugars

Ingredients

1 pound pork rind raw, scored by the butcher

1 tablespoon sea salt

2 tablespoon smoked paprika

Directions

Sprinkle and rub salt on the skin side of the pork rind. Allow it to sit for 30 minutes.

Roast at 380 degrees F for 8 minutes; turn them over and cook for a further 8 minutes or until blistered.

Sprinkle the smoked paprika all over the pork scratchings and serve. Bon appétit!

Salted Pretzel Crescents

(Ready in about 20 minutes | Servings 4)

Per serving: 273 Calories; 16.3g Fat; 23.7g Carbs; 6.6g Protein; 4.4g Sugars

Ingredients

1 can crescent rolls

10 cups water

1/2 cup baking soda

1 egg, whisked with 1 tablespoon water

1 tablespoon poppy seeds

2 tablespoons sesame seed

1 teaspoon coarse sea salt

Directions

Unroll the dough onto your work surface; separate into 8 triangles.

In a large saucepan, bring the water and baking soda to a boil over high heat.

Cook each roll for 30 seconds. Remove from the water using a slotted spoon; place on a kitchen towel to drain.

Repeat with the remaining rolls. Now, brush the tops with the egg wash; sprinkle each roll with the poppy seeds, sesame seed and coarse sea salt. Cover and let rest for 10 minutes.

Arrange the pretzels in the lightly greased Air Fryer basket.

Bake in the preheated Air Fryer at 340 degrees for 7 minutes or until golden brown. Bon appétit!

Mozzarella Stick Nachos

(Ready in about 40 minutes | Servings 4)

Per serving: 551 Calories; 28.7g Fat; 36.3g Carbs; 39.1g Protein; 1.7g Sugars

Ingredients

1 (16-ounce) package mozzarella cheese sticks

2 eggs

1/2 cup flour

1/2 (7 12-ounce) bag multigrain tortilla chips, crushed

1 teaspoon garlic powder

1 teaspoon dried oregano

1/2 cup salsa, preferably homemade

Directions

Set up your breading station. Put the flour into a shallow bowl; beat the eggs in another shallow bowl; in a third bowl, mix the crushed tortilla chips, garlic powder, and oregano.

Coat the mozzarella sticks lightly with flour, followed by the egg, and then the tortilla chips mixture. Place in your freezer for 30 minutes.

Place the breaded cheese sticks in the lightly greased Air Fryer basket. Cook at 380 degrees F for 6 minutes.

Serve with salsa on the side and enjoy!

Easy Fried Button Mushrooms

(Ready in about 15 minutes | Servings 4)
Per serving: 259 Calories; 4.3g Fat; 47.5g Carbs; 8.7g Protein; 2.4g Sugars

Ingredients

1 pound button mushrooms

1 cup cornstarch

1 cup all-purpose flour

1/2 teaspoon baking powder

2 eggs, whisked

2 cups seasoned breadcrumbs

1/2 teaspoon salt

2 tablespoons fresh parsley leaves, roughly chopped

Directions

Pat the mushrooms dry with a paper towel.

To begin, set up your breading station. Mix the cornstarch, flour, and baking powder in a shallow dish. In a separate dish, whisk the eggs.

Finally, place your breadcrumbs and salt in a third dish.

Start by dredging the mushrooms in the flour mixture; then, dip them into the eggs. Press your mushrooms into the breadcrumbs, coating evenly. Spritz the Air Fryer basket with cooking oil. Add the mushrooms and cook at 400 degrees F for 6 minutes, flipping them halfway through the cooking time.

Serve garnished with fresh parsley leaves. Bon appétit!

Party Pancake Kabobs

(Ready in about 40 minutes | Servings 4)
Per serving: 292 Calories; 6.5g Fat; 53.1g Carbs; 5.6g Protein; 23.1g Sugars

Ingredients

Pancakes:

1 cup all-purpose flour

1 teaspoon baking powder

1 tablespoon sugar

1/4 teaspoon salt

1 large egg, beaten

1/2 cup milk

1/2 teaspoon vanilla extract

2 tablespoons unsalted butter, melted

Kabobs:

1 banana, diced

1 Granny Smith apples, diced

1/4 cup maple syrup, for serving

Directions

Mix all ingredients for the pancakes until creamy and fluffy. Let it stand for 20 minutes.

Spritz the Air Fryer baking pan with cooking spray. Drop the pancake batter on the pan with a small spoon.

Cook at 230 degrees F for 4 minutes or until golden brown. Repeat with the remaining batter. Tread the mini pancakes and the fruit onto bamboo skewers, alternating between the mini pancakes and fruit.

Drizzle maple syrup all over the kabobs and serve immediately.

Mini Bread Puddings with Cinnamon Glaze

(Ready in about 50 minutes | Servings 5)

Per serving: 435 Calories; 23.1g Fat; 49.6g Carbs; 9g Protein; 28.1g Sugars

Ingredients

5 tablespoons butter

1/2 pound cinnamon-raisin bread, cubed

1 cup milk

1/2 cup double cream

2/3 cup sugar

1 tablespoon honey

1 teaspoon pure vanilla extract

2 eggs, lightly beaten

Cinnamon Glaze:

1/4 cup powdered sugar

1 teaspoon ground cinnamon

1 tablespoon milk

1/2 teaspoon vanilla

Directions

Begin by preheating your Air Fryer to 370 degrees F. Lightly butter five ramekins.

Place the bread cubes in the greased ramekins. In a mixing bowl, thoroughly combine the milk, double cream, sugar, honey, vanilla, and eggs.

Pour the custard over the bread cubes. Let it stand for 30 minutes, occasionally pressing with a wide spatula to submerge.

Cook in the preheated Air Fryer at 370 degrees F degrees for 7 minutes; check to ensure even cooking and cook an additional 5 to 6 minutes.

Meanwhile, prepare the glaze by whisking the powdered sugar, cinnamon, milk, and vanilla until smooth. Top the bread puddings with the glaze and serve at room temperature. Bon appétit!

Easy Zucchini Chips

(Ready in about 20 minutes | Servings 4)

Per serving: 154 Calories; 5.9g Fat; 14.7g Carbs; 8.5g Protein; 2.2g Sugars

Ingredients

3/4 pound zucchini, peeled and sliced

1 egg, lightly beaten

1/2 cup seasoned breadcrumbs

1/2 cup parmesan cheese, preferably freshly grated

Directions

Pat the zucchini dry with a kitchen towel.

In a mixing dish, thoroughly combine the egg, breadcrumbs, and cheese. Then, coat the zucchini slices with the breadcrumb mixture.

Cook in the preheated Air Fryer at 400 degrees F for 9 minutes, shaking the basket halfway through the cooking time.

Work in batches until the chips is golden brown. Bon appétit!

Creamed Asparagus and Egg Salad

(Ready in about 25 minutes + chilling time | Servings 4)

Per serving: 245 Calories; 22.9g Fat; 5.3g Carbs; 6g Protein; 2.4g Sugars

Ingredients

2 eggs

1 pound asparagus, chopped

2 cup baby spinach

1/2 cup mayonnaise

1 teaspoon mustard

1 teaspoon fresh lemon juice

Sea salt and ground black pepper, to taste

Directions

Place the wire rack in the Air Fryer basket; lower the eggs onto the wire rack.

Cook at 270 degrees F for 15 minutes.

Transfer them to an ice-cold water bath to stop the cooking. Peel the eggs under cold running water; coarsely chop the hard-boiled eggs and set aside.

Increase the temperature to 400 degrees F. Place your asparagus in the lightly greased Air Fryer basket.

Cook for 5 minutes or until tender. Place in a nice salad bowl. Add the baby spinach.

In a mixing dish, thoroughly combine the remaining ingredients. Drizzle this dressing over the asparagus in the salad bowl and top with the chopped eggs. Bon appétit!

Roasted Green Bean Salad with Goat Cheese

(Ready in about 10 minutes + chilling time | Servings 4)

Per serving: 296 Calories; 24.3g Fat; 11.1g Carbs; 10.3g Protein; 3.9g Sugars

Ingredients

1 pound trimmed green beans, cut into bite-sized pieces
Salt and freshly cracked mixed pepper, to taste
1 shallot, thinly sliced
1 tablespoon lime juice
1 tablespoon champagne vinegar
1/4 cup extra-virgin olive oil
1/2 teaspoon mustard seeds
1/2 teaspoon celery seeds
1 tablespoon fresh basil leaves, chopped
1 tablespoon fresh parsley leaves
1 cup goat cheese, crumbled

Directions

Toss the green beans with salt and pepper in a lightly greased Air Fryer basket.

Cook in the preheated Air Fryer at 400 degrees F for 5 minutes or until tender.

Add the shallots and gently stir to combine.

In a mixing bowl, whisk the lime juice, vinegar, olive oil, and spices. Dress the salad and top with the goat cheese. Serve at room temperature or chilled. Enjoy!

Red Currant Cupcakes

(Ready in about 20 minutes | Servings 3)

Per serving: 346 Calories; 8.5g Fat; 58.9g Carbs; 8.7g Protein; 22.2g Sugars

Ingredients

1 cup all-purpose flour
1/2 cup sugar
1 teaspoon baking powder
A pinch of kosher salt
A pinch of grated nutmeg
1/4 cup coconut, oil melted
1 egg
1/4 cup full-fat coconut milk
1/4 teaspoon ground cardamom
1/4 teaspoon ground cinnamon
1 teaspoon vanilla extract
6 ounces red currants

Directions

Mix the flour with the sugar, baking powder, salt, and nutmeg. In a separate bowl, whisk the coconut oil, egg, milk, cardamom, cinnamon, and vanilla.

Add the egg mixture to the dry ingredients; mix to combine well.

Now, fold in the red currants; gently stir to combine. Scrape the batter into lightly greased 6 standard-size muffin cups.

Bake your cupcakes at 360 degrees F for 12 minutes or until the tops are golden brown. Sprinkle some extra icing sugar over the top of each muffin if desired. Enjoy!

Scrambled Egg Muffins with Cheese

(Ready in about 20 minutes | Servings 6)
Per serving: 286 Calories; 19.9g Fat; 6.8g Carbs; 19.6g Protein; 2.4g Sugars

Ingredients

6 ounces smoked turkey sausage, chopped
6 eggs, lightly beaten
2 tablespoons shallots, finely chopped
2 garlic cloves, minced
Sea salt and ground black pepper, to taste
1 teaspoon cayenne pepper
6 ounces Monterey Jack cheese, shredded

Directions

Simply combine the sausage, eggs, shallots, garlic, salt, black pepper, and cayenne pepper in a mixing dish. Mix to combine well.

Spoon the mixture into 6 standard-size muffin cups with paper liners.

Bake in the preheated Air Fryer at 340 degrees F for 8 minutes. Top with the cheese and bake an additional 8 minutes. Enjoy!

Spring Chocolate Doughnuts

(Ready in about 20 minutes | Servings 6)
Per serving: 345 Calories; 11.6g Fat; 56g Carbs; 6.1g Protein; 22.8g Sugars

Ingredients

1 can (16-ounce) can buttermilk biscuits
Chocolate Glaze:
1 cup powdered sugar
4 tablespoons unsweetened baking cocoa

2 tablespoon butter, melted
2 tablespoons milk

Directions

Bake your biscuits in the preheated Air Fryer at 350 degrees F for 8 minutes, flipping them halfway through the cooking time.

While the biscuits are baking, make the glaze.

Beat the ingredients with whisk until smooth, adding enough milk for the desired consistency; set aside.

Dip your doughnuts into the chocolate glaze and transfer to a cooling rack to set. Bon appétit!

Sweet Mini Monkey Rolls

(Ready in about 25 minutes | Servings 6)
Per serving: 446 Calories; 23.7g Fat; 54.1g Carbs; 5.3g Protein; 22.5g Sugars

Ingredients

3/4 cup brown sugar
1 stick butter, melted
1/4 cup granulated sugar
1 teaspoon ground cinnamon
1/4 teaspoon ground cardamom
1 (16-ounce) can refrigerated buttermilk biscuit dough

Directions

Spritz 6 standard-size muffin cups with nonstick spray. Mix the brown sugar and butter; divide the mixture between muffin cups.

Mix the granulated sugar with cinnamon and cardamom. Separate the dough into 16 biscuits; cut each in 6 pieces. Roll the pieces over the cinnamon sugar mixture to coat. Divide between muffin cups.

Bake at 340 degrees F for about 20 minutes or until golden brown. Turn upside down and serve.

Cranberry Cornbread Muffins

(Ready in about 35 minutes | Servings 4)

Per serving: 439 Calories; 18.2g Fat; 60.9g Carbs; 8.2g Protein; 19.7g Sugars

Ingredients

3/4 cup all-purpose flour

3/4 cup cornmeal

1 teaspoon baking powder

1/2 teaspoon baking soda

1/2 teaspoon salt

3 tablespoons honey

1 egg, well whisked

1/4 cup olive oil

3/4 cup milk

1/2 cup fresh cranberries, roughly chopped

Directions

In a mixing dish, thoroughly combine the flour, cornmeal, baking powder, baking soda, and salt. In a separate bowl, mix the honey, egg, olive oil, and milk.

Next, stir the liquid mixture into the dry ingredients; mix to combine well. Fold in the fresh cranberries and stir to combine well.

Pour the batter into a lightly greased muffin tin; cover with aluminum foil and poke tiny little holes all over the foil. Now, bake for 15 minutes. Remove the foil and bake for 10 minutes more. Transfer to a wire rack to cool slightly before cutting and serving. Bon appétit!

Hanukkah Latkes (Jewish Potato Pancakes)

(Ready in about 20 minutes | Servings 4)

Per serving: 384 Calories; 2.7g Fat; 79g Carbs; 12.3g Protein; 7.8g Sugars

Ingredients

6 potatoes

4 onions

2 eggs, beaten

Sea salt and ground black pepper, to taste

1/2 teaspoon smoked paprika

1/2 cup all-purpose flour

Directions

Pulse the potatoes and onions in your food processor until smooth. Drain the mixture well and stir in the other ingredients. Mix to combine well.

Drop the pancake batter on the baking pan with a small spoon. Flatten them slightly so the center can cook.

Cook at 370 degrees for 5 minutes; turn over and cook for a further 5 minutes. Repeat with the additional batter.

Serve with sour cream if desired.

Crispy Wontons with Asian Dipping Sauce

(Ready in about 20 minutes | Servings 4)

Per serving: 335 Calories; 11.7g Fat; 28.1g Carbs; 27.2g Protein; 4.5g Sugars

Ingredients

1 teaspoon sesame oil

3/4 pound ground beef

Sea salt, to taste

1/4 teaspoon Sichuan pepper

20 wonton wrappers

Dipping Sauce:

2 tablespoons low-sodium soy sauce

1 tablespoon honey

1 teaspoon Gochujang

1 teaspoon rice wine vinegar

1/2 teaspoon sesame oil

Directions

Heat 1 teaspoon of sesame oil in a wok over medium-high heat. Cook the ground beef until no longer pink. Season with salt and Sichuan pepper.

Lay a piece of the wonton wrapper on your palm; add the beef mixture in the middle of the wrapper. Then, fold it up to form a triangle; pinch the edges to seal tightly.

Place your wontons in the lightly greased Air Fryer basket. Cook in the preheated Air Fryer at 360 degrees F for 10 minutes. Work in batches.

Meanwhile, mix all ingredients for the sauce. Serve warm.

Oatmeal Pizza Cups

(Ready in about 30 minutes | Servings 4)

Per serving: 343 Calories; 12.8g Fat; 35.6g Carbs; 22.4g Protein; 7.2g Sugars

Ingredients

1 cup rolled oats
1 teaspoon baking powder
1/4 teaspoon ground black pepper
Salt, to taste
2 tablespoons butter, melted
1 cup milk
4 slices smoked ham, chopped
4 ounces mozzarella cheese, shredded
 4 tablespoons ketchup

Directions

Start by preheating your Air Fryer to 350 degrees F. Now, lightly grease a muffin tin with nonstick spray.

Pulse the rolled oats, baking powder, pepper, and salt in your food processor until the mixture looks like coarse meal.

Add the remaining ingredients and stir to combine well. Spoon the mixture into the prepared muffin tin.

Bake in the preheated Air Fryer for 20 minutes until a toothpick inserted comes out clean. Bon appétit!

RECIPE INDEX

Classic Egg Salad 121
Classic Fried Pickles 59
Classic Italian Arancini 82
Classic Onion Rings 67
Classic Vanilla Mini Cheesecakes 107
Classic Vegan Chili 96
Cocktail Cranberry Meatballs 71
Cocktail Party Fruit Kabobs 110
Coconut Chip Cookies 113
Coconut Shrimp with Orange Sauce 53
Cod and Shallot Frittata 50
Corn on the Cob with Herb Butter 62
Country Pie with Walnuts 110
Country-Style Apple Fries 119
Couscous with Sun-Dried Tomatoes 99
Crab Cake Burgers 52
Cranberry Cornbread Muffins 133
Creamed Asparagus and Egg Salad 130
Crème Brûlée French Toast 91
Creole Turkey with Peppers 23
Crispy Butternut Squash Fries 94
Crispy Mustardy Fish Fingers 57
Crispy Tilapia Fillets 51
Crispy Wontons with Asian Dipping Sauce 133
Crunch-Crunch Party Mix 127
Crunchy Broccoli Fries 72
Crunchy Eggplant Rounds 95
Crunchy Munchy Chicken Tenders with Peanuts 15
Crustless Beef and Cheese Tart 38

D

Dad's Roasted Pepper Salad 96
Delicious Hot Fruit Bake 116
Delicious Snapper en Papillote 54
Delicious Turkey Sammies 85
Dessert French Toast with Blackberries 104
Dijon Roasted Sausage and Carrots 20
Dijon Top Chuck with Herbs 36

Dilled and Glazed Salmon Steaks 55

E

Easiest Vegan Burrito Ever 126
Easy Blueberry Muffins 109
Easy Chocolate and Coconut Cake 113
Easy Chocolate Brownies 108
Easy Crispy Shawarma Chickpeas 94
Easy Fried Button Mushrooms 129
Easy Frittata with Mozzarella and Kale 117
Easy Granola with Raisins and Nuts 99
Easy Greek Revithokeftedes 114
Easy Hot Chicken Drumsticks 15
Easy Keto Pork Rinds 34
Easy Lobster Tails 49
Easy Pork & Parmesan Meatballs 26
Easy Pork Sandwiches 32
Easy Prawns alla Parmigiana 55
Easy Ritzy Chicken Nuggets 17
Easy Roasted Hot Dogs 125
Easy Sweet Potato Bake 61
Easy Sweet Potato Hash Browns 64
Easy Veggie Fried Balls 59
Easy Zucchini Chips 130
Egg Noodles with Sausage-Pepper Sauce 33
English Muffins with a Twist 125
English-Style Flounder Fillets 50

F

Famous Blooming Onion with Mayo Dip 73
Famous Buffalo Cauliflower 95
Famous Western Eggs 124
Farmer's Breakfast Deviled Eggs 114
Favorite Apple Crisp 106
Favorite Cheese Biscuits 85
Favorite Spinach Cheese Pie 89
Fingerling Potatoes with Cashew Sauce 115
French Toast with Blueberries and Honey 123
Fried Green Beans with Pecorino Romano 60
Fried Peppers with Sriracha Mayo 59

Fried Pickle Chips with Greek Yogurt Dip 77
Fruit Skewers with a Greek Flair 116

G
Garden Vegetable and Chicken Casserole 22
Garlic-Roasted Brussels Sprouts with Mustard 101
Gourmet Wasabi Popcorn 102
Grandma's Butter Cookies 105
Greek-Style Pizza with Spinach and Feta 90
Greek-Style Roast Fish 57
Greek-Style Roasted Figs 121
Greek-Style Roasted Tomatoes with Feta 67
Greek-Style Squash Chips 80
Greek-Style Vegetable Bake 68
Green Beans with Oyster Mushrooms 102
Green Pea Fritters with Parsley Yogurt Dip 119
Grilled Cheese Sandwich 119
Grilled London Broil with Mustard 43
Grilled Salmon Steaks 51
Ground Pork and Cheese Casserole 27

H
Halibut Cakes with Horseradish Mayo 54
Hanukkah Latkes (Jewish Potato Pancakes) 133
Herb Roasted Potatoes and Peppers 103
Herbed Pork Loin with Carrot Chips 26
Hibachi-Style Fried Rice 81
Hoisin-Glazed Bok Choy 103
Homemade Beef Empanadas 43
Homemade Pork Scratchings 128

I
Indian Famous Fish Curry 55
Indian Plantain Chips (Kerala Neenthram) 100
Indonesian Beef with Peanut Sauce 44
Italian Chicken and Cheese Frittata 20
Italian Panettone Bread Pudding 81
Italian Sausage and Veggie Bake 121
Italian-Style Honey Roasted Pork 27

Italian-Style Risi e Bisi 101

J
Jamaican Cornmeal Pudding 117
Japanese Chicken and Rice Salad 86
Japanese Tempura Bowl 69

K
Kale Chips with Tahini Sauce 73
Kid-Friendly Mini Meatloaves 40
Korean-Style Breakfast Patties 42
Korean-Style Salmon Patties 49

L
Lemon-Basil Turkey Breast 21
Light and Fluffy Chocolate Cake 109

M
Mayonnaise and Rosemary Grilled Steak 40
Meatballs with Cranberry Sauce 39
Mediterranean Chicken Breasts with Roasted Tomatoes 16
Mediterranean Roasted Vegetable and Bean Salad 126
Mediterranean Vegetable Skewers 63
Mediterranean-Style Beef Steak and Zucchini 36
Mexican Cheesy Zucchini Bites 79
Mexican-Style Brown Rice Casserole 86
Mexican-Style Corn on the Cob with Bacon 70
Mexican-Style Ground Pork with Peppers 27
Mini Bread Puddings with Cinnamon Glaze 130
Mocha Chocolate Espresso Cake 112
Monkfish with Sautéed Vegetables and Olives 53
Moroccan-Style Steak Salad 47
Mother's Day Pudding 117
Mozzarella Stick Nachos 128

N

New York Strip with Mustard Butter 37
New York Strip with Pearl Onions 42
New York-Style Pizza 84

O

Oatmeal Pizza Cups 134
Old Bay Calamari 56
Old-Fashioned Chicken Drumettes 17
Ooey-Gooey Dessert Quesadilla 98

P

Paella-Style Spanish Rice 91
Paprika Chicken Legs with Brussels Sprouts 18
Paprika Potato Chips 72
Parsnip Chips with Spicy Citrus Aioli 76
Party Pancake Kabobs 129
Peperonata with Beef Sausage 36
Peppermint Chocolate Cheesecake 106
Perfect Sloppy Joes 32
Philadelphia Mushroom Omelet 114
Polenta Fries with Sriracha Sauce 83
Pork Belly with New Potatoes 29
Pork Cutlets with a Twist 25
Pork Koftas with Yoghurt Sauce 24
Pork Loin with Mushroom Sauce 33
Pork Shoulder with Molasses Sauce 28
Pretzel Crusted Chicken with Spicy Mustard Sauce 14
Pretzel Knots with Cumin Seeds 85
Puerto Rican Tostones 77
Puff Pastry Meat Strudel 91

Q

Quick Sausage and Veggie Sandwiches 40
Quick-Fix Seafood Breakfast 58
Quinoa with Baked Eggs and Bacon 124

R

Rainbow Roasted Vegetables 93
Rainbow Vegetable Fritters 63
Ranch Parmesan Chicken Wings 21

Red Currant Cupcakes 131
Rich Couscous Salad with Goat Cheese 88
Risotto Balls with Bacon and Corn 87
Roasted Broccoli with Sesame Seeds 62
Roasted Cauliflower Florets 75
Roasted Citrus Turkey Drumsticks 22
Roasted Green Bean Salad with Goat Cheese 131
Roasted Parsnip Sticks with Salted Caramel 79
Roasted Ribeye with Garlic Mayo 37
Roasted Veggies with Yogurt-Tahini Sauce 63
Rosemary Roasted Mixed Nuts 115
Rum Roasted Cherries 126
Rustic Baked Apples 111
Rustic Chicken Legs with Turnip Chips 17
Rustic Pizza with Ground Pork 24

S

Salted Pretzel Crescents 128
Saucy Garam Masala Fish 51
Sausage and Mushroom Chili 34
Savory Cheese and Herb Biscuits 89
Savory Italian Crespelle 118
Scotch Fillet with Sweet 'n' Sticky Sauce 37
Scrambled Egg Muffins with Cheese 132
Scrambled Eggs with Sausage 122
Skinny Pumpkin Chips 65
Smoked Halibut and Eggs in Brioche 52
Smoked Salmon and Rice Rollups 82
Smoked Sausage with Sauerkraut 30
Smoky Mini Meatloaves with Cheese 29
Snapper Casserole with Gruyere Cheese 58
Southwest Bean Potpie 122
Spicy Bacon-Wrapped Tater Tots 25
Spicy Curried King Prawns 49
Spicy Glazed Carrots 61
Spicy Roasted Potatoes 60
Spicy Seafood Risotto 83
Spring Chocolate Doughnuts 132

Sticky Dijon Pork Chops 33

StLouis-Style Pork Ribs with Roasted Peppers 35

Summer Meatballs with Cheese 20

Sunday Banana Chocolate Cookies 111

Sunday Glazed Cinnamon Rolls 88

Sunday Tender Skirt Steak 44

Sweet Corn Fritters with Avocado 67

Sweet Mini Monkey Rolls 132

Sweet Potato Chips with Greek Yogurt Dip 66

Sweet Potato Fries with Spicy Dip 72

Swiss Chard and Potato Fritters 97

Swiss Cheese & Vegetable Casserole 64

T

Taco Stuffed Bread 84

Tarragon Turkey Tenderloins with Baby Potatoes 16

Tender Marinated Flank Steak 41

Tender Spare Ribs 29

Teriyaki Chicken Drumettes 78

Thai Red Duck with Candy Onion 16

Thai Sweet Potato Balls 99

Thanksgiving Turkey Tenderloin with Gravy 22

The Best Calamari Appetizer 77

The Best Cauliflower Tater Tots 65

The Best Crispy Tofu 93

The Best Fish Tacos Ever 89

The Ultimate Berry Crumble 111

Three-Cheese Stuffed Mushrooms 66

Thyme-Roasted Sweet Potatoes 74

Tofu in Sweet & Sour Sauce 101

Tortilla-Crusted Haddock Fillets 48

Traditional Onion Bhaji 118

Tuna Steaks with Pearl Onions 48

Turkey Bacon with Scrambled Eggs 19

V

Veggie Casserole with Ham and Baked Eggs 123

Veggie Fajitas with Simple Guacamole 97

Vermouth and Garlic Shrimp Skewers 48

W

Wonton Sausage Appetizers 71

CPSIA information can be obtained
at www.ICGtesting.com
Printed in the USA
BVHW011422140722
642159BV00007B/168